Copyright © 2013 by Miquel Hudin and Èlia Varela Serra
First edition published by Leavenworth Press, May 2013
All rights reserved.

Design by Clara Juan and Roser Cerdà

"Vinologue" is a registered trademark.

All rights reserved. No part of this publication may be reproduced, stored in a retrieval system or transmitted in any form, or by any means, electronic, mechanical, photocopying, recording, or otherwise, without the prior written permission of the copyright owner(s).

Disclaimer

While every effort has been made to ensure accuracy, the author and publisher will not be liable for any inconvenience or loss resulting from possible inaccuracies. Information such as contact details, maps, and routes may have changed and the publisher would appreciate updated information. Please write to: info@vinologue.net

All photographs were taken by Miquel Hudin and Èlia Varela Serra with the exception of pages: 97, 119, 122, 123, 155, 161, 165, 191, 220, 222, 273, 275, 316, 318, 343, 359 which were provided by the wineries.

Cover Photo: The terraces of Torres Priorat in El Lloar.
Author Photo by Valentí Llagostera

ISBN: 97-809-83771-852
DL: B.10612-2013

Printed by Liberdúplex in Catalonia, Spain

Vinologue Priorat

A regional guide to enotourism in Catalonia including 104 producers and 315 wines

Index

General Info **9**
Introduction. 11
Icons 13
Practical Information. 14
History of Priorat Wine. 20
Defining DOQ Priorat. 23
Local Varietals 26
Llicorella. 30
Local Specialties 31
Regional Events. 34
Suggested Itineraries. 37

Zones **41**
La Morera, Escaladei, Les Vilelles 43
Torroja del Priorat. 49
Poboleda 53
Porrera. 59
Gratallops. 65
El Lloar, El Molar 71
Bellmunt del Priorat, Falset 75

Cellers. **81**
Celler de L'Abadia 83
Agnès de Cervera. 85
Agrícola de Poboleda 89
Aixalà Alcait. 93
Álvaro Palacios 97
Ardèvol i Associats. 103
Arrels del Priorat 105
Balaguer i Cabré 107
Balmaprat. 111
Bartolomé. 113
Els Bigotis del Gat 115
Blai Ferré Just 117
Buil & Giné. 119
Bujorn 123
Cal Pla 125
Capafons-Ossó 129
Cartoixa de Montsalvat. 133
Casa Gran del Siurana 135

Castellet	139
Cecilio	141
Cesca Vicent	145
Cims de Porrera	149
Clos 93	153
Clos Berenguer	155
Clos Dominic	157
Clos Erasmus	161
Clos Figueras	165
Clos Mogador	169
Clos de l'Obac	175
Clos del Portal	179
La Conreria d'Scala Dei	183
Costers del Priorat	187
Les Cousins	191
Cristian Francés Breton	193
De Muller	195
Devinssi	199
Domaines Magrez Espagne	203
Domini de la Cartoixa	205
Celler de l'Encastell	207
Escoda Pallejà	211
Família Nin-Ortiz	213
Ferrer Bobet	217
Finca Tobella	221
Franck Massard	225
Genium Celler	227
Gran Clos	231
Gratavinum	235
Heid & Marqués	239
Hidalgo Albert	241
L'Infernal	245
Joan Ametller	249
Joan Simó	253
Lo	257
Llicorella Vins	259
Maius	263
Marco Abella	265
Mas Alta	269
Mas Basté	273
Mas d'en Blei	275
Mas Doix	279
Mas Garrian	283
Mas d'en Gil	287
Mas Igneus	291

Mas Martinet	295
Mas la Mola	299
Mas Perinet	303
Mas Perla	307
Mas Sinén	309
Mayol	313
Melis	317
Meritxell Pallejà	319
Morlanda	321
Noguerals	325
Pasanau	327
La Perla del Priorat	331
Pinord Mas Blanc	337
Pins Vers	341
Piñol i Sabaté	343
Celler del Pont	345
Prior Pons	347
Puig Priorat	349
RAR	353
Ripoll Sans	355
Roca de les Dotze	359
Rotllan Torra	361
Sabaté	365
Sabaté Franquet	369
Sabaté i Mur	371
Sangenís i Vaqué	373
Saó del Coster	377
Sara i René Viticultors	381
Cellers de Scala Dei	383
Sedó Barceló	389
Solà Clàssic	393
T41	397
Tane	399
Terra de Verema	403
Terroir al Límit	407
Torres Priorat	413
Trosset	417
Trossos del Priorat	419
Vall Llach	423
Vinícola del Priorat	427
Vinya del Vuit	431

Special Thanks

The authors would like to thank the following people for helping to make this book possible: Marta Domènech for instigating this whole affair and aiding visits to elusive wineries, Ruth Troyano for encouraging us from the start, Yuri & Ferran Mestres for their limitless knowledge of Priorat history, Eva Escudé for connecting countless dots, Mireia Pujol-Busquets for helping us be Gratallops-based during research of this guide, Sílvia of Forn del Pi for being our helpful landlady and the unofficial tourism office of Gratallops, Jaume Balaguer Vicent for his wealth of information on Priorat cellars big and small, Pati Vega for wifi and sustenance, Marc Aguiló for random requests, Salvador Burgos for being the consumate Poboleda insider, Jaume Josa and the DOQ Priorat office for fact-checking assistance, Cathryn Hudin for support, and the Varela Serra family for a list of things that are too many to fully enumerate.

General Info

Introduction
What is this guide?

Icons

Practical Information
When to Go
Getting There & Back
Hotel Options
Traveling with Wine
Communication
Catalan Language

History

Defining DOQ Priorat
Vi de la Vila

Local Varietals

Llicorella

Local Specialties

Regional Events

Itineraries

Introduction

DOQ Priorat. As one of only two wine regions in Spain to gain the very exclusive "Qualified" adjective in its official name, it's no wonder that their wines are known the world over.

Winemaking can be traced back 800 years or more when Carthusian monks from France decided to set up shop in the area. In the centuries the followed, people eked out a living on the steep hills and rocky slopes. Then, a revolution of modern winemaking started 30 years ago that brought Priorat out in to the international spotlight. Of course, it came with a reputation of strong bodied, expensive wines.

The 2008 global financial collapse hit Priorat exceptionally hard given that they, like other Spanish regions, exported the vast majority of their bottles outside of the country. As if this wasn't enough, there was also a slowly changing taste preference in wine drinkers for more food-friendly wines with less oak and concentration, which had been a key characteristic of the wines for years.

The 100 or so cellars did what their grapevines do in an adverse environment, they dug in. They went back to what it is that has made the Priorat wines great: the terrain, locale, and countless old wine vines dotting those steep hills and terraces. Born of this thinking is a new focus on showing one grape varietal and letting it speak from the bottle with the most minimal of intervention. As one winemaker in Priorat likes to say, "the enologs should be the vines".

But, beyond the bottles they're making, it's also the case that more wineries have opened up their doors for visitors. Whereas just a handful of wineries welcomed people to come and taste 10 years ago, now a great majority of them do. They want people who visit to experience the land-

← **Vines and the Ebre Valley seen from Bellmunt**

scape and understand how labor intensive their wines are to make and the amount of patient hand work that goes in to producing each bottle.

There are few places where it's possible to see vines literally growing out of rocks on slopes so steep that you can barely walk on them. The villages are quiet and tranquil, completely free of the development that happened on the coast just 30 minutes south or east. This is no Napa Valley. There are no tour buses or limousines flying around the twisty roads. Visits are intimate, authentic, and now, more than ever is the time for a wine lover to enjoy a truly unique experience.

What is this guide? Flip open your favorite travel guide for Spain and within 400 or so pages, you'll find 2-3 that talk about the wines. This guide takes the opposite approach and makes the wine the destination.

It's presented as a simple, immediately approachable guide to the wine region of Priorat. It's full of all the wineries that visitors will encounter, information on their tastings, how to get there, and GPS coordinates.

You'll note that there are no scores for the wines because, what does a number tell you? Maybe your wine with a score of 10, or 20, or 100 is much different than someone else's, and especially than a critic who spends 30 seconds or less on a wine and ends up spitting it out. To that end, descriptive tasting notes are included to help guide you through the different wines and find those that may be your style, or those that best fit a certain situation. But these are just a starting point. Go wild, try everything and maybe find a new bottle or grape you never knew you'd love.

Please note that all reviews are unsolicited and not paid for by the wineries covered. Tastings were conducted on the premises everywhere it was possible and as any reader would experience them.

Winery Icons

They accept visitors on a regular basis throughout the year. You may still need to make an appointment, so read the information section closely.

They either don't accept visits from the general public or do so in a very limited fashion, seasonally, or on a case by case basis.

The winery either has staff members or can arrange translation to English and other languages in addition to Catalan & Spanish.

Larger groups of 12 or more visitors can easily be accommodated on the premises.

A maker of "Flying Wine" in that while their wines are certified by DOQ Priorat, they don't own a cellar and rent facilities.

A winery with all or part of their vineyards fully certified organic and/or biodynamic. Read their profile for exact details.

Those with mobility impairments should be able to visits these wineries, but call ahead to verify, especially for restrooms.

Wine Icons

A wine that represents an excellent balance of price and quality within the scope of the region.

A wine with the stringent "Vi de la Vila" certification. Read about the full description of this in the Defining DOQ Priorat section.

Vinologue authors personally recommend this wine based on a number of factors including its unique character and taste.

Wine Types

- Rosé
- White
- Red
- Dessert or other types

Practical Information

Spain and Catalonia have invested a great deal in being very tourist friendly. The tourist office for the entire Priorat region is located next to the Consell Comarcal building behind the city hall on the main square in Falset. Unfortunately, they're only open in the morning except for Saturday. Additionally, they have an extensive website in multiple languages to help aid visitors in planning their stay, including a calendar of events and a list of tour agencies.
www.turismepriorat.org

Guides For those who wish to have a guided trip to the region, there are many tour operators based in Barcelona who offer a "Priorat package". While convenient, the best experience for visitors will be had through local guides. The tourism office in Priorat can help you to find one, although if you don't speak Catalan or Spanish they'll most likely just put you in contact with Rachel Ritchie. Although originally British, she's lived in Priorat for years, is intimately familiar with the region, its wines, and is not only fluent in Catalan and Spanish but seems to speak every European language in existence including English, French, and German.

Alternatively, if you want to experience more of the nature of Priorat combining hiking with winery visits, contact El Brogit. They offer a variety of trips that take visitors through the historic trails of the Priorat with stopovers at local wineries. Another option is CatSud, based in Falset.
www.rachelritchie.com, www.elbrogit.com, www.catsud.com

When to Go

The general rule of thumb for any time of the year is to call beforehand to make sure it's a good time for the cellar as the vast majority are small without a specific person assigned to visitors. Some prefer visits during weekends as they live elsewhere or they are in the fields during the week, while others will prefer weekdays.

While by definition wineries run year-round, there are indeed times that are more ideal than others. December, January and February are typically the worst as it is incredibly cold and most people go out as little as possible.

March through May is a much better time. While there may be rain, the weather is warmer and life comes back to the cellars and vineyards, with lots of flowers and trees blossoming. The best time, if you're able to deal with a pinch of heat is June, July, and early September. August can be decent, but people are often at the beach as the temperatures are incredibly hot.

Harvest (late September through October) can be the best and the worst time to visit. Some wineries don't take visitors during this time as they're incredibly busy, working 16-hour days, every day of the week. Others are more than happy to have visitors as it allows people to see the winery in full swing, and a handful of them even offer harvest-related activities. November is quite nice, but many people take off a week or two given how intense the harvest is.

Getting There & Back

Plane Most people arriving internationally will land in Barcelona's El Prat airport. From there, a local train or the Aerobus take people to the Barcelona city center. As an alternative, there is the Reus airport just 25km away from Priorat. The primary carrier is the budget airline, Ryanair with a connecting bus once an hour to the center of Reus.

Car Rental Rental cars are plentiful in this tourist-friendly part of the world, although you need to keep in mind that the alcohol limit for driving is 0.05%. There are also many, many police checkpoints as well as portable radar speed detectors during the high season and holiday weekends, so make sure to designate a driver and watch the speed. Cars are also not cheap to rent in the high season and will put a huge dent in your budget. But, to visit most of the wineries on your own, they're completely necessary. Just remember that there are only two gas stations in the region: Falset and Cornudella de Montsant.

While it's possible to hire a car in Barcelona, it's also possible in Reus (both in the center and at the airport) for those wishing to avoid the drive in and out of Catalonia's sprawling capital city. Make sure reserve online ahead of time to save money and ensure you get a car.

Train & Bus Amazingly, despite the small size and remoteness to the villages, it is possible to visit Priorat without a car. It isn't easy though. The train arrives from Barcelona at the Marçà-Falset station. From there, a shuttle bus runs the route between the station and the town of Falset. At just 2.5km from town, one can also walk or ride a bicycle.

To get to the wineries, there are several local bus routes that run through most of the main villages in the comarca. The schedules aren't terribly frequent, but they can work to have a few decent visits. Consult the main bus website, walk up to the main depot on the north side of Falset, or ask at the tourism office.
www.renfe.com, www20.gencat.cat/portal/site/mobilitat

Alternatively, you can rent a bicycle in Barcelona's wealth of bike rental shops and take it with you in the train. However, bear in mind that while distances in Priorat are short, the roads are twisty and often steep once you leave Falset.

Cal Llop in Gratallops

Hotel Options

There are several hotel options in Priorat worthy to note. The largest and most classic is Hostal Sport in Falset which has both a hotel and restaurant. There are smaller hotels around the villages that are noted in the village sections.

Beyond hotels though, the most common lodging option are the "casa rurals". These are old homes in rural areas that have been renovated to accept guests with one of the most well-known being Cal Compte in Torroja.
www.casesrurals.com

Traveling with Wine

More than likely, when visiting wineries you will buy a bottle... or maybe 12 of something you like. With shipping costs for wine costing more than the wine itself, how do you take it home with you? One trick is to wrap the bottles in the dirty clothes in your suitcase. It is indeed possible that a bottle could still break, but keep in mind that bottles are quite strong. The key is to make sure that they don't have direct contact with one another, but read up:
www.enotourist.net/traveling-with-wine/

Winery Communication

All methods to contact wineries are listed in their profiles. Most have functioning email accounts and some (not many) are fantastic with responding while others make you feel like your message fell in to a digital black hole. If you don't hear a response a day or two after sending a message, try the phone number listed.

Telephone numbers in Spain are comprised of nine digits and the international country code is +34. Fixed lines start with a 9 and more specifically in Priorat, they start with 977. Mobile phones typically start with a 6 and will be more expensive to call from a land line.

Catalan Language

Catalonia wasn't always a part of Spain. It was its own kingdom for centuries and then a joint, but equal kingdom with neighboring Aragon for several more. But, on September 11, 1714 Barcelona fell in the War of Succession and for the last 300 years, it has been, much to the chagrin of the Catalans, under the Spanish Crown. There have been attempts to establish an independent Catalonia throughout this time, but none have managed to succeed.

Territorial Organization

As Catalonia is administratively part of Spain, first-time visitors are often under the impression that Catalan is a dialect of Spanish. While Latin-based, it's a Romance language in its own right and is as related to Spanish (or Castilian, as it's called in Spain) as Spanish is to Italian or to Portuguese. Want further proof? Take the simple example of "a sandwich with ham and cheese". In Spanish this is, "un bocadillo con jamón y queso". In Catalan, it's "un entrepà amb pernil i formatge".

Catalan is the only official language of Andorra and a co-official language with Castilian in the Spanish autonomous communities of Catalonia, the Balearic Islands, and Valencia. It is also spoken in the historic northern Catalan region of Roussillon in southern France. Since education in Catalonia is in both Spanish and Catalan, most everyone in the region is completely bilingual and you will have no problem communicating in Spanish with the Catalan winemakers listed in this guide. But, as you will see, towns, streets, and grapes are all written with Catalan spellings.

Note that Catalan has two main dialects, Eastern and Western, with differences in pronunciation. The Priorat dialect is the Western variant and differs a bit from the one spoken in Barcelona.

For those wishing to delve further in to the language, you will be met with open arms by the Catalans, who appreciate outsider interest in their language as it is looked upon with annoyance by Castilian speakers. There are books you can buy such as "Teach Yourself Catalan" by Alan Yates and Anna Poch or "Catalan: A Comprehensive Grammar" by Max Wheeler.

Online resources:
www.parla.cat
www.wikipedia.org/wiki/Catalan_grammar
en.wikivoyage.org/wiki/Catalan_phrasebook

To learn more:
en.wikipedia.org/wiki/Catalan_language
en.wikipedia.org/wiki/History_of_the_Catalan_language

History of Priorat Wine

First Period: Antiquity – 1163
The initial history of wine in Priorat can be dated back to Roman times. The capital of this region was Tarragona which was a day's journey to the east of Priorat. While the Romans (and the Greeks before them) had been producing wine in Catalonia, there isn't any definitive evidence that it was being produced in Priorat. There are many ruins scattered about the region that can be dated back to the Roman period however and it's generally safe to assume that they were producing some amount of wines there.

In the 8th century, the region fell under Moorish, Muslim control which put a stop to any winemaking in the region. It would remain under their control until the 12th century only be completely "re-conquered" with the final taking of the high mountain village of Siurana in 1153, marking the end of Moorish control in Catalonia.

Second Period: 1163 – 1835
It's the later 12th century where things start to get interesting again in terms of wine. In 1163, Alfons el Cast founded "Cartoixa de Santa Maria d'Escaladei" establishing the first Carthusian monastery in the Iberian Peninsula. The location in a secluded valley by the Montsant bluff was where a shepherd had a vision of angels climbing a staircase to heaven, thus the name, "scala dei" or "stairs to god".

Naturally, where Christian monks go, the wine shall follow. The lands that were established around the monastery became the priory or, in Catalan, "priorat" and all the villages in the region became heavily integrated in to the monks' winemaking. Throughout the 13th to the early 17th century, the power and wealth of this monastery grew immensely as they gained control of more lands, mines, and became a feudal lord of the region. They also sent out monks to many other regions in Iberia to establish more monasteries.

All was not well though and the people of the region grew weary of the heavy taxes and tributes they had to pay to the monastic order. The monastery's lands were initially stripped in 1820, but returned three years later to only then see them completely and finally stripped by the 1835 Ecclesiastical Confiscations of Mendizábal. This Spain-wide privatization of church lands that were largely unused saw the end of many centuries-old orders.

The local residents in Priorat, tools in hand, took a great deal of pleasure in sacking and destroying the monastery. The ruined state it sits in today is not due to centuries of sun and rain, but the peasantry taking out their aggression on what they saw to be an oppressive landlord.

Third Period: 1835 – 1979
Winemaking continued on a smaller scale after the end of the monastery and in 1893, the phylloxera plague found its way south from France. It first started in the village of Porrera, but by the end of the 19th century, it had decimated every single vine of the 5,000 hectares in the region.

Most people finally gave up on the harsh environment, threw in the proverbial towel, and left for cities like Tarragona or Barcelona. Those who stayed had to replant their vines. They found safety in numbers though and formed cooperatives to make their wines together to share facilities and risk. The only problem in this is that, like other regions in Catalonia, they were most interested in large production and as such, planted a great amount of Carignan vines due to its robust production. As a native grape to the region, Grenache was also replanted, but it was the Carignan that was seen to be the breadwinner.

In the 1970s Cellers de Scala Dei (something of a modern inheritor to the old monastic vineyards and cellar) started producing wines in a more controlled, French style. These caught the eye of people from outside Priorat.

Fourth Period: 1979 – 2008

René Barbier III, as the descendent of a French winemaking family that had been in Catalonia for some time, came to Priorat in 1979 and started planting vines on terraces and rehabilitating other, older vines. He planted French varietals such as Cabernet Sauvignon, Merlot, and Syrah that had previously been unseen there. He also convinced others in the wine business to come with him.

While there was initially a larger group that came to try their hand, four others remained with René Barbier in the end and resulted in the wineries of Clos Mogador by René, Mas Martinet by Josep Lluís Pérez, Clos Erasmus by Daphne Glorian, Clos de l'Obac by Carles Pastrana and Mariona Jarqué, and of course Álvaro Palacios who initially called his wines, Clos Dofí. The wines this Big Five created gained international attention and awards which in turn drove more people to come to Priorat and start new wineries. In the early 1990s, there were just 15 registered wineries with the DOQ body, whereas these days there are 100.

The old Carignan vines planted for high production and the Grenache planted for hardiness showed that with age and reserved cultivation, they made some stunningly elegant bottles. The wines continued to escalate in fame and demand around the world throughout the 1990s and in to the 2000s.

Fifth Period: 2008 - ?

Many things happened to make 2008 one of the tougher years the winemakers in Priorat had seen in a long, long time. While most all regions in Spain heavily export their wines internationally, Priorat wineries exported upwards of 85% of their production. When the dust of the 2007-2008 Financial Crisis settled, the world wine markets were heavily shaken. With a massive decrease in wealth, wine sales around the world plummeted, including Priorat.

A few small wineries stopped bottling their vintages and went back to selling grapes to the larger producers, much like they were in the early 20th century. Others realized that they would have to show what it is that has been historically unique about Priorat to make their wines stand out from an increasingly crowded wine market.

This has seen winemakers start to make single varietal wines to show how amazing those old Carignan and Grenache vines are when left to their own devices with minimal technological intervention. Winemakers are also dialing back the degree of oak in the wines as tastes in general are shifting away from these strong, potent wines that had garnered so many points a couple of decades ago.

As to what the future holds, it's impossible to guess given that the harvests of 2011 and 2012 were with little rain and quite low in production volumes. But, if Priorat is anything, it's resilient and most likely this is just one more storm that will pass its stony hills throughout the centuries.

Defining DOQ Priorat

With its foundations dating back to the 17th century, Spain established a formal Denominación de Origen (or DO) structure for wine in the 1920s, although it was revised several times throughout the 20th century to arrive in 1996 at the system in place today. There are currently 12 official DO certifications issued within the territory of Catalonia.

The DO, at its core is a system of quality control. It exists in a similar form in both France and Italy. Given that terms such as "artisanal" carry little official weight, the DO acts as a regulation body to ensure that wine as well as food meets a set of standards set forth by semi-autonomous governing bodies. They inspect wineries to ensure that compliance is met and they issue labels for winemakers to affix to their bottles to denote certification. They control the types of grapes that can be used, the geographic area where the grapes can be sourced from as well as how the wines must be aged and stored.

For some this may come as a foreign concept. For example there is no equivalent body in the US. Even though the American Viticultural Area, or AVA designation of regions exists there, it isn't in any way comparable to the regulation system of the DO and has no certification element.

The wines in this guide are certified by the DOQ Priorat which was established in 1954 (albeit without the Q initially) with offices initially located in Reus, about 30km outside the actual region before they moved to the village of Torroja del Priorat in 1999. The name, "Priorat" is protected and all wines that are certified with this label must be grown and produced within the boundaries of the DOQ region. It doesn't cover all municipalities in the Priorat comarca but only 11 (12 if Escaladei is counted separately from La Morera del Montsant) with a total surface area of about 20,000 hectares; the vineyards covering about 10% of that. There are currently about 100 certified wineries and countless other producers who rent space at one of these wineries (and who appear in this guide as "flying wineries"). The total production of all the wineries and producers certified by the DOQ Priorat is round 5 million liters.

As of 1985, all certified wines must be bottled with no bulk sales permitted for certification and only a select list of grapes allowed in the wines. Additionally, the regulations cover how the grapes are grown with a maximum of 6,000kg of grapes allowed per hectare although on average it's usually half of this. In the case of the "Vi de finca" certification, the allowed yield is 15% less. Grapes should be picked by hand, not mechanically harvested and the harvest boxes must hold less than 20kg in weight. The maximum density of vines per hectare is 9,000 and the minimum is 2,500 with only 12 buds allowed per vine. Once the grapes are harvested, they should only be pressed gently with no more than 65 liters per 100kg being allowed.

There are many, many more regulations that are quite stringent up until the wine is tasted by a committee of experts. All of this is in the name of creating high quality wines. This is an important distinction to make as Priorat is one of only two regions in all of Spain to have a "Q" after DO (the other being Rioja). This stands for "Qualified" ("qualificada" in Catalan, "calificada" in Spanish) and they were granted this certification in 2000 for consistently producing very high quality wines.

Vi de la Vila
This was an initiative spearheaded in 2009 by Álvaro Palacios to create an even more finite system of demarcation for the wines from the region, specifying the exact village and vineyard where the grapes grew. All of the 11 municipalities the DOQ covers have the option to produce wines certified as being only from within their boundaries including: Bellmunt del Priorat, Escaladei, Gratallops, El Lloar, La Morera del Montsant, Poboleda, Torroja del Priorat, La Vilella Alta, La Vilella Baixa, Masos del Falset, and Solanes del Molar.

A wine must be at least 60% Carignan, Grenache or both (considered the two native grapes of Priorat) and produced in the same village from where the grapes are harvested. It's but one part of the group of initiatives by winemakers in the region to show what it is that's great and unique about their wines.

Local Varietals

As several of the grapes that the wineries in Priorat use are actually native to the region, they have different names than those used in English—which are often just derived from the French names. Below is a chart comparing the names in a variety of languages for easy reference.

English	Catalan /Castilian
Carignan	Samsó, Carinyena / Cariñena, Mazuela
Grenache	Garnatxa, Lledoner / Garnacha
Hairy Grenache	Garnatxa Peluda / Garnacha Peluda
Chenin Blanc	Xenin Blanc / Chenin Blanc
Malvasia	Malvasia / Malvasía
Macabeu	Macabeu / Macabeo, Viura
Piquepoul	Picapoll / Picapoll
Tempranillo	Ull de Llebre /Tempranillo
Muscat	Moscatell / Moscatel

There are officially 18 varietals allowed for wine production in DOQ Priorat with five of those being preferred and seen as best suited for the region. A wine must list a maximum of five varietals on the label unless one comprises less than 5% of the finished blend.

White Grapes
Grenache, Macabeu, Pedro Ximénez, Chenin Blanc, Muscat of Alexandria, Muscat Blanc à Petits Grains, Piquepoul, Xarel·lo (locally known as Pansal)

Red Grapes
Recommended: Grenache, Carignan
Permitted: Hairy Grenache, Cabernet Sauvignon, Cabernet Franc, Tempranillo, Piquepoul, Pinot Noir, Merlot, Syrah

Carignan

Known in Spanish as Cariñena and in Catalan as either Carinyena or Samsó, this grape is thought to originally be from the Cariñena area in the Aragón region of Spain that's immediately west of Catalonia. It has been grown in Catalonia for as long anyone can remember and is actually rarely found in Cariñena these days. It's in France where it gained a rather horrible reputation as a grape given that in the Languedoc-Roussillon region they planted it to over-produce. The results were rather unfortunate, sharp wines and many of these vines have since been torn out.

In Priorat, there is a great wealth of old growth Carignan vineyards and they produce wonderfully mature and subtle wines that can age for years. It still requires a great deal of skill to produce these wines and the best vines are usually found on the old, steep slopes that are plentiful about the region.

The name in Catalan of Samsó can be confusing, though, as in French there is a different grape called Cinsault which sounds nearly identical. The Catalans have used Samsó primarily to avoid confusion with the DO Cariñena region, as the term Cariñena/Carinyena is protected by that DO. Several wineries in Priorat don't care for the Samsó name which they feel is artificial and simply write the grape as the intentionally misspelled "Caranyena".

Grenache

Known as Garnacha in Spanish and Garnatxa or Lledoner in Catalan, this grape is heavily planted across the region. They make heavy use of both the red and white variants which have established themselves as workhorse grapes for Catalonia as a whole. Despite the French name that is used in English, it is very much a Catalan grape. While it gained popularity in neighboring Aragón, it grows fantastically well in Priorat.

Full bodied and throaty, yet elegant, as a red it is typically blended with Carignan, although a good number of single varietal bottles of Red Grenache are easy to find. As a white grape it is also robust and loves to toss out all manner of minerality that allows it to be blended quite well with Macabeu.

Hairy Grenache

It's often the case that Garnatxa Peluda (Garnacha Peluda) gets lumped in to just being yet another type of Grenache. Whether it's a separate type or not is something of a moot point as it is a distinctly different grape than standard Grenache. The name which means, "Hairy Grenache" is due to the downy undersides of leaves that evolved to protect the vine from transpiration in the heat, conserve moisture and reduce stress. The grapes also have considerably thicker skins and it is a rather hardy grape, particularly resistant to high winds.

It can have a wonderful, massive bouquet with dark aspects such as anise and fennel. But it generally has lower alcohol and very little body and as such is blended with "regular" Grenache grapes or others with more depth to them.

Escanyavella

This is an old grape in Priorat that literally translates as, "Old Lady Strangler" from Catalan. The name probably referred to it being a strong grape and making people cough when drinking it, which is still true to some degree in regards to the raw grape.

It's sometimes considered to be the same grape as Merseguera, but DNA profiling carried out by the Catalan Wine Institute has shown that it is a distinct, singular grape.

It can be minerally with good aromatic herbs, acidity, and freshness. Overall, it's a quite pleasant grape and it can be found in small amounts in many white wines from Priorat. Only one winery, Ripoll Sans, makes a wine that's 100% from this grape.

Macabeu

This white grape is apparently originally from the Valencia region, but has been widely planted in Catalonia as well as in Rioja where it acquired the less commonly used name of Viura. It is never found as a single varietal wine in Priorat. Macabeu is quite popular to use in a blend with White Grenache to create a very nicely balanced bottle.

Singularly, it typically has floral aspects to the nose and is rather light in the body.

Pedro Ximénez

The fame of this grape is generally more tied to its use in Sherry from the south of Spain than in white wines, but it's actually common to find it bottled in a non-Sherry setting. The origin of its name is thought to be originally from the Canary Islands, but there is little evidence to support this, although the grape itself could indeed be from the islands. Whatever the origin, it's been grown a great deal in Spain for the last few centuries and perhaps even more.

When bottled as a white wine, it has undeservedly gained the reputation of making a poor wine. As is often the case with generalizations, this is not the case, especially when seen in Priorat where the region has boosted the strength of this grape so much that you often see it bottled as a single varietal.

While generally light, the wines can display a good degree of minerality along with a nice freshness. It can even take well to barrel aging that helps promote all these enjoyable aspects of the grape.

Llicorella

"Llicorella" or "llacorell" is a type of rock that defines a great deal of what Priorat is. Walking out in the old, sloped vineyards, it will crumble under your feet, but somehow, the grape vines grow out of it.

For all technical purposes, llicorella is a type of slate that is mixed with quartz and dates from the Paleozoic era. It is very porous and doesn't retain water well. This attribute makes it all but impossible to grow anything in it except for grape vines that dig their roots down to 24 meters in order to gain access to water.

This soil is most everywhere in the region, except in the south which is composed much more of clay. In the sun, it shimmers and throughout the year, it maintains heat, which works to ripen the grapes. It puts such a signature stamp on the wines that many of the wineries have one of their wines named after the soil. One winery even named themselves after this soil. Suffice to say, Priorat would not be what it is without the llicorella.

Local Specialties

Avellanes
These are not specifically from Priorat, but the hazelnuts grown in the Tarragona area are famous all over Spain and like no other hazelnut you've tried. The same hard growing conditions that make great wines also make great nuts and these are rich, buttery in flavor, and insanely addictive.

Cóc/Coca de Recapte
There are endless variations of coca in Catalonia, called cóc in the Tarragona area, which basically means flatbread. Many of them are sweet, but the vegetable ones are the most interesting. Some may find them similar to pizza, but their origin is older and didn't use to have a tomato base. They're typically made with seasonal toppings and not much else other than bread, but these days it's common to find llonganissa sausage or tuna versions. For Saint Blaise on February 3rd, several meter long coques are paraded around the streets of Falset and eaten afterwards.

Clotxa
In a similar way as coca de recapte, clotxa was traditionally eaten while working in the fields. It is a round loaf of bread that has been emptied and filled with sardines or herrings and grilled vegetables.

Mel de Gratallops
While not known for its honey, several beekeepers have started producing from hives in the area. Salvador Sorroche in Gratallops was at the forefront of this in Priorat, making all sorts of honeys from beehives placed by specific herbs in the region. These can be found at his shop in Gratallops near the entrance to the village and across the street from Forn del Pi. One not to miss is the "Cap d'ase" honey, made with a type of local lavender called "donkey head". In his shop you can also find his insanely delicious honey chocolate as well as other honey-based products.

Menjablanc
Menjablanc or menjarblanc (literally, "white meal") is an ancient, simple custard dessert made primarily from almond milk, a touch of lemon peel, sugar and cinnamon. Authentic versions are topped with the hazelnuts. Local legend says it became popularized by a monk in Scala Dei.

Olives
Wine gets all the glory, but the olives are glorious. They can be found in a multitude of locations. Most bars and restaurants will have them as a snack and most any shop with a few groceries will sell them.

Olive oil
All the olive oil produced in the Priorat comarca falls under the protected denomination of Siurana, that certifies its quality. It is of extremely high quality, very aromatic, and simply delicious. Almost all of it made with Arbequina olives, although some producers like Miró Cubells make oils with other local varieties such as rojals. His Cavaloca oil has won numerous awards and can be found at the family shop in Escaladei next to Cellers de Scala Dei. They also do oil tastings at the shop and offer visits of their oil press in Cabacés. And check out "Oli del raig" which is a first press olive oil made only at the very start of the olive harvest.

Truita amb Suc

Truita is the Catalan name for an omelet, called "tortilla" in Spanish (not to be confused with the flour or corn tortilla from Mexico). This specific variation on the dish is "juicy" in that some sauce is added to the truita to turn it into a main dish. There are many variations on this omelet, some with spinach, others with beans, but they're all delicious. You'll often find them at local festivals and Ulldemolins even puts on an event in March devoted entirely to it.

Vermut

This is an old tradition that has seen a resurgence in the rest of Catalonia lately, but never went out of style in southern regions such as Priorat. To put it succinctly, it's a pre-meal snack paired with a Vermut, a local wine-based drink that has a bitter component to it that whets the appetite. If this sounds familiar to Vermouth, it's because it is. The Catalan take on it sees people eating a couple of olives, chips, and other small bites along with a small glass of the drink. You haven't really experienced Priorat unless you've made sure to fit a Vermut in to your Sunday. A number of the wineries in the area make a Vermut wine and it's definitely worth a taste.

Regional Events

May is typically the busiest month for wine-related events in all of Priorat, although there are a few others throughout the year:

Priorat Wine Fair in Falset
The first weekend in May, Falset fills up with people for the largest wine fair of the Priorat region. Wineries from both DOQ Priorat and DO Montsant offer tastings at the fair but also at many parallel events around town. It presents a fantastic opportunity for visitors to taste everything from the region in a very festive environment. If you're planning to go, book your accommodation well ahead as 15,000+ people descend on the region for this event.
www.firadelvi.org

Carignan Night in Porrera
On the first weekend of May, the wineries in Porrera organize a dinner and tasting of their Carignan wines. The majority of them will go into blends, so it's a unique opportunity to taste all that this grape has to offer in the specific locale of the Porrera area.
www.cellersdeporrera.com

Tast amb llops
During the wine fair in Falset, the owners of Cal Llop in Gratallops organize a tasting of local wines in the square in front of their hotel.
www.tastambllops.com

Tast de les mines
This is a tasting held at the Mine Museum in Bellmunt del Priorat at the beginning of May. What's interesting about it is that it's a vertical tasting of several wineries not only in Bellmunt but also in El Lloar and El Molar.

Tast de Cal Compte
During the wine fair in Falset, the owners of Cal Compte in Torroja organize a tasting of local wines in the square in front of their hotel.
www.tastdecalcalcompte.com

Tast de vins del Lloar i Les Solanes d'El Molar
At the beginning of August, the DOQ Priorat wineries within the El Lloar and El Molar municipalities showcase their wines.

Wine Night in Torroja
At the end of August, all the wineries in Torroja offer a tasting of their wines under the stars.
www.torroja.altanet.org

Ancient Grape Harvest Festival in Poboleda
Since 1999, on the second or third Saturday of September, Poboleda pays tribute to the way the grape harvest was done in the old days. Everyone in town dresses in traditional costumes and goes together to the vineyards to harvest. The whole town is decorated and several activities show old tools and techniques. Wine tastings are also on the program and wineries from all over DOQ Priorat are present. The weekend before the fair, Poboleda wineries open their doors to visitors free of charge.

In April, Poboleda hosts a tasting for professionals of the wines they produce under the name "Poboleda Vins".
www.poboleda.oasi.org

Vin Blanc Festival
This festival held in La Morera at the beginning of November honors a type of young sweet wine called, "vin blanc". Very unique to the region, it's a rare opportunity to taste several of them made by local winemakers as well as their regular wines.
www.lamorerademontsant.org

Tasta Porrera
In the second weekend of November, during the winter festa major for Porrera, they hold their annual tasting event for all of the wineries in the village. It's a great time for tasting the wines as well as regional food dishes prepared by all the restaurants in Porrera.
www.cellersdeporrera.com

Tast de Santa Bàrbara
Held at the beginning of December in Bellmunt del Priorat during their patron saint festivities, it's a tasting of the young wines not yet bottled from the wineries in town.
www.bellmunt.altanet.org

Festes Majors
Every village in Priorat celebrates a "festa major", which is a festival honoring the local patron saint. They usually involve some kind of musical acts, activities for children, and of course gastronomic and wine fairs with tastings. Some villages, like Porrera, even have more than one festa major. To find out the exact dates and program of each festa major, visit the Priorat Tourism website or ask at the office they have in Falset.
www.turismepriorat.org

Suggested Itineraries

To decide which of the 100+ Priorat wineries to visit in a short period of time can be a daunting endeavor. The following are a few suggested schedules for people wishing to visit the region for two days or a weekend. These serve merely as a starting point though and within each of the sub regions in the following chapter, one day options are given as well. Note that most if not all wineries require prior reservations for visits, so reference the wineries section in the guide to plan accordingly.

Priorat Highlights

Start out the day by making a visit to the **Escaladei Monastery** to see where it all began. Follow up this visit with a tasting at **Cellers de Scala Dei** in the village. Enjoy a lunch of traditional Catalan dishes at **El Rebost**. In the afternoon, head to **Mas Doix** in Poboleda for a tasting and visit to their vineyards. Head down to Porrera and spend the night in **Hotel els Pampols**.

The next morning pay a visit to **Clos Dominic** to see their old vineyards and taste their wines. For lunch, head down to Gratallops and try local Priorat specialties at **El Piró** restaurant. If you want to take some wine home, make sure to visit their wine shop next door featuring most of the wineries in Priorat. In the afternoon, visit **Clos Mogador** to experience one of the original wineries of the "new" Priorat. Either head home in the evening or spend a night at **Hostal Sport** in Falset, making sure to enjoy their fantastic classic dinner options, or go to **Celler del'Àspic** for more modern/experimental dining.

Wilderness & Wine

Start out with a morning hike in the **Montsant** bluff by taking the trailhead in La Morera. Have lunch in La Morera at **Balcó del Priorat**. In the afternoon, pay a visit to Pasanau winery. Head down to Torroja and enjoy dinner at **Cal Joc** and spend the night at **Cal Compte**.

In the morning, go for a walk through the vineyards on the other side of the valley from the village. Then head to Gratallops and hike up to the **Ermita de la Consolació** to enjoy the spectacular views with lunch afterwards at **La Cassola** or **La Font** and a visit to **Ripoll Sans** in the afternoon and if you find you have open time, pop in to **Buil & Giné** in Gratallops. Or, drive to Poboleda, have lunch at **El Cau** and then walk or drive out to **Mas Sinén** to experience their organic wines and warm hospitality. Just make sure to visit the **Ermita de Sant Gregori** near Falset at sunset.

Enjoy the Ride, Leave the Car

As stated, earlier, you can visit Priorat without a car, but it requires planning and you're best off being based in Falset. Call **Capafons-Ossó** to arrange a visit and let them know when you're arriving so they can pick you up at the nearby **Marçà-Falset train station**. Enjoy the visit of their winery in the morning. Afterwards have them drop you off at **Hostal Sport** to leave your bags and enjoy lunch. In the afternoon, catch the local bus to Torroja to visit **Aixalà Alcait**, **Llicorella Vins**, or **L'Infernal**. Take the bus back to Falset and have dinner at **El Cairat** or **Cellar de l'Àspic**.

In the morning, after the traditional "esmorzar amb forquilla" breakfast at **Hostal Sport**, take the local bus up to Gratallops and visit **Saó del Coster**. For lunch, enjoy **El Piró** or, if on a budget, a quick sandwich at **Cal Llens** followed by a glass of wine at the cooperative, **Vinícola del Priorat's** well-stocked shop. In the afternoon, stop in at **Cecilio**, **Devinssi**, or both for a taste. Or, take the short walk up the road to **Trossos del Priorat** for a visit and tasting. Just make sure that whichever option you choose, leave enough time to catch the local bus back to Falset. If you get stuck in Gratallops, you could always spend a night at **Cal Llop**, a boutique hotel in a renovated old stone house in the center of town that also has a good restaurant.

Whether spending another night in Falset (and having a drink at wine bar, **Calaix de Sastre**) or leaving the same evening, check the bus schedule back to the train station to coordinate it with the train as there are only 5-6 a day.

Zones

La Morera del Montsant, Escaladei, Les Vilelles

Torroja del Priorat

Poboleda

Porrera

Gratallops

El Lloar, El Molar

Bellmunt del Priorat, Falset

WINERIES

1. Joan Ametller
2. Pasanau
3. Cellers de Scala Dei
4. La Conreria d'Scala Dei
5. Masia Duch
6. Cartoixa de Montsalvant
7. Terra de Verema
8. Vinyes Altair
9. Mas Alta
10. Bujorn
11. Sabaté
12. Celler del Pont
13. Lo

WINE SHOPS

1. La Vinateria del Boli

SITES

1. Escaladei Monastery
2. Montsant Natural Park

AMENITIES

1. Balcó del Priorat
2. El Rebost
3. La Plaça
4. Els Troncs
5. Lo Cupet 39
6. L'Abadia
7. Cal Centro
8. Agrobotiga
9. El Racó
10. Cal Pep

- Municipality
- River
- Road
- Secondary road
- Wineries
- Sites
- Amenities
- Wine Shops

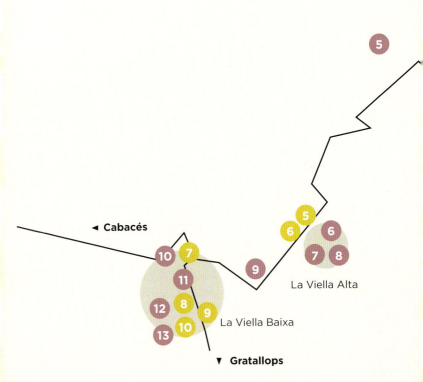

La Morera, Escaladei, La Vilella Alta, La Vilella Baixa

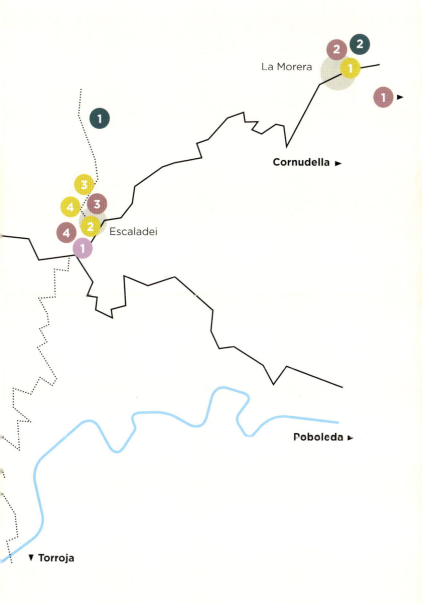

La Morera del Montsant

Morera-Escaladei-Vilelles

La Morera de Montsant
Up from Escaladei is the highest village in the region, La Morera de Montsant which essentially kisses the cliffs. With a striking view and a couple of wineries, it makes for a pleasant day visit. It's also an excellent point to enter the **Montsant Natural Park** (2) trailhead for whatever level of hiking and climbing desired. If hiking and wine fires up the appetite, stop in to **el Balcó del Priorat** (1) for a meal or to spend the night as they offer rooms as well.

Escaladei
This corner of the region is the most significantly historic due to the Carthusian monks initially setting up shop back in the 12th century. The small stone village is not much more than a handful of buildings but it has the restaurants of **El Rebost** (2), **La Plaça** (3), and **Els Troncs** (4). Each of them offers a fixed price lunch menu that's a good value.

Of course, the main attraction is the **Escaladei Monastery** (1) and museum which is located about one kilometer past the village. It's an impressive stop with some portions heavily restored and others still being worked on. If for some reason, you reach it and it's closed, walk up the dirt road on the left. While you can't see everything from there, it does offer an impressive glimpse. That same dirt road is also another access point for hiking in the Montsant Natural Park (2).

La Vilella Alta
Down the road from Escaladei, sits La Vilella Alta. It's a small, scenic village with a couple of wineries on the south side of it as well as the restaurants **Lo Cupet 39** (5) which is one of the better values in fixed price menus in the area. **L'Abadia** (6) has rooms for rent.

La Vilella Baixa
Further along the road is La Vilella Baixa which the villagers have proclaimed to be the "Manhattan of Priorat" due to its tall houses by the river. There is no way to state this except ironically as while Manhattan is the city that never sleeps, La Vilella Baixa seems to be the one that never truly wakes up. The quiet is part of the charm though, as well as how the whole village is seemingly perched on a rocky point. In addition to the wineries, there are also the restaurants of **El Racó** (9) and **Cal Pep** (10). El Racó has great traditional food and a good value lunch menu on weekdays, but the service can seriously test your patience at times. It also has five rooms to rent.

At the **Agrobotiga** (8) of the Vinícola del Priorat it's possible to buy the high quality regional olive oils directly as well as many of the Priorat wines. Local oils and wines can also be bought at the shop of the winery **Sabaté** (11). A great shop for local meats and other tasty food items is next door, **Cal Centro** (7) where you can also sit down for coffee and a snack.

Suggested Itinerary

Starting out the day with a visit to the **Escaladei Monastery** is a great way to see the historical parts of how Priorat came to be. Stopping in at either **Cellers Scala Dei** or **La Conreria d'Scala Dei** afterwards offers the opportunity to see how the winemaking in the area has evolved.

Grab lunch at either **El Rebost** in Escaladei or **Lo Cupet 39** in La Vilella Alta. After lunch take in another one of the Escaladei wineries if you didn't get to visit both in the morning and then head up to **Pasanau** in La Morera for a tasting and watch the sun set over Priorat.

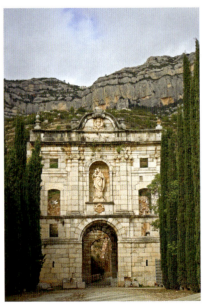

Escaladei Monastery

Contacts

L'Abadia
977839477, 659424031
Plaça de la Vila, 3
La Vilella Alta

Agrobotiga
977839272
Carrer Nou
La Vilella Baixa

Balcó del Priorat
977827211
Bonrepòs, 17
La Morera de Montsant

Cal Centro
977839378
Carrer Nou, 2
La Vilella Baixa

Cal Pep
977839454
Priorat, 12 bis
La Vilella Baixa

Lo Cupet 39
977839086, 636361963
Carrer Major
La Vilella Alta

La Plaça
977827327
Plaça del Priorat, 6
Escaladei

El Racó
977839065, 618144992
Priorat, 9
La Vielella Baixa

El Rebost
977827149
Rambla Cartoixa, 15
Escaladei

Els Troncs
977827158
Rambla Cartoixa, 10
Escaladei

La Vinateria del Boli
977827194
Carrer Mitja Galta, 28
Escaladei
www.vinateria-boli.com

WINERIES

1. L'Infernal
2. Llicorella Vins
3. Sabaté Franquet
4. Sabaté i Mur
5. Aixalà Alcait
6. Rotllan Torra
7. Heid & Marqués
8. Mayol
9. Escoda Pallejà
10. Terroir al Límit
11. DOQ Priorat Office

AMENITIES

1. Cal Joc
2. Cal Compte

- Municipality
- River
- Road
- Secondary road
- Wineries
- Sites
- Amenities
- Wine Shops

▲ **Escaladei**

◀ **Gratallops**

Torroja

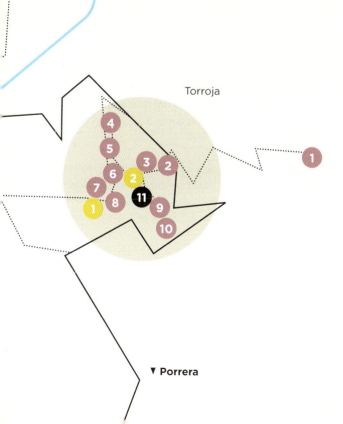

Torroja del Priorat

This village in the center of Priorat has its founding recorded in 1261. The name is derived from a portmanteau of "torre" and "roja" that referred to the large red watchtower which existed historically. It's a wonderfully picturesque village that seems to hover out above the valley where it's located, keeping watch on the Siurana River below and the vineyards that border it. One of the most preserved villages in the region, it is essentially the "San Francisco" to La Vilella Baixa's "Manhattan" as walking through this small village of less than 200 inhabitants requires going up and down the small hills a bit.

Packed with 10 of the region's wineries, including some of the best, the village is also home to the **DOQ Priorat offices** (11). They can provide visitors with some materials for visiting the wineries, although their primary function is to administer their wine jurisdiction.

For dining needs as well as wireless internet, **Cal Joc** (1) is the spot. In addition to their lunch menu and general café offer, they also have a small store at the front of their restaurant to buy meats, cheeses, and other local products including all of the wines from Torroja. They even have wine-related jewelry made with llicorella stones by the extremely friendly owner, Pati Vega.

For those looking to enjoy a very classy stay in Priorat, check out **Cal Compte** (2) which is a gorgeous eight bedroom hotel in a fully renovated 18th century village house.

Suggested Itinerary
Start with a visit to **Aixalà Alcait** in the morning. Enjoy the affordable fixed price lunch at **Cal Joc**. In the afternoon, visit **Llicorella Vins** and, if time permits, **L'Infernal** at the end of the very end of the day to catch the sun setting across Torroja.

Contacts

Cal Joc
977839182, 649283592
Carrer de la Brasa, 9
Torroja del Priorat
www.caljoc.cat

Cal Compte
619023779
Carrer Major, 4
Torroja del Priorat
www.calcompte.com

Passage below Cal Compte

WINERIES

1. Tane
2. Noguerals
3. Maius
4. Mas Perinet
5. Mas d'en Blei
6. Terres de Vidalba
7. Pahí
8. Mas Doix
9. Agrícola de Poboleda
10. Mas d'en Just
11. Mas la Mola
12. Genium
13. Jordi Domènech
14. Hidalgo Albert
15. Mas de les Pereres
16. Mas Sinén

SITES

1. Siurana

AMENITIES

1. El Cau
2. Casal la Closa
3. Els Cups / Hostal Populetus
4. Càmping Poboleda
5. Cal Carles
6. Porta del Priorat
7. Venta del Pubill

- Municipality
- River
- Road
- Secondary road
- Wineries
- Sites
- Amenities
- Wine Shops

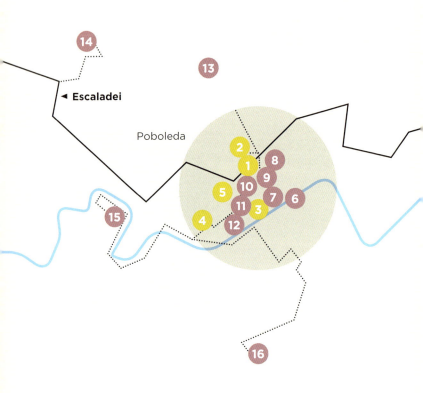

Poboleda

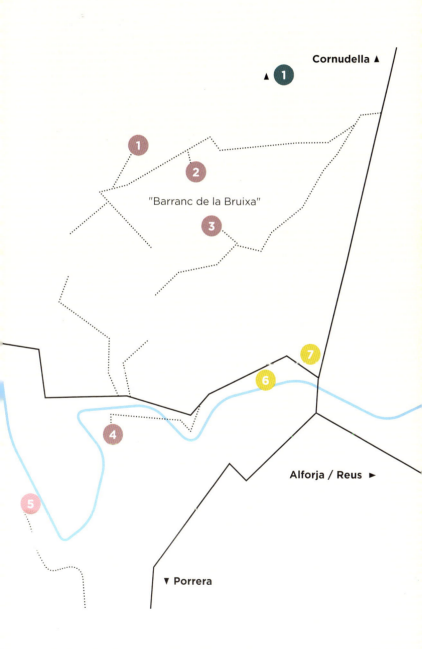

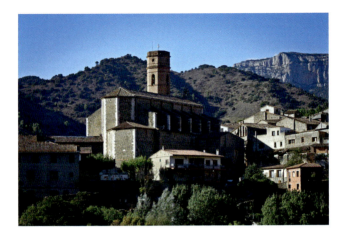

Poboleda

There are documents showing the existence of Poboleda at least back to the 12th century and its name is thought to be derived from Latin meaning "forest of poplars". Much like the other villages in the center of Priorat, it's in a very well preserved state with old stone houses lining two central streets that end at the church and the Siurana River flowing and twisting alongside the village.

While not the furthest northern village in Priorat, it gives a sense of being rather self contained with 16 wineries in close proximity to it. Despite having a bit less than 400 residents, it has several places to eat. In town are **El Cau** (1), **Casal la Closa** (2), and **Els Cups** (3). A bit to the east are **Porta del Priorat** (6) and **Venta del Pubill** (7). El Cau is especially welcoming with its fixed price lunch menus and seasonal Catalan dishes. Venta del Pubill isn't noteworthy for its food so much as it's a popular geographic marker.

Staying in Poboleda is also quite comfortable with the affordable option of **Càmping Poboleda** (4) during the warmer months and the more traditional options of Hostal **Populetus** (3) and the casa rural of **Cal Carles** (5).

If taking the time to visit Poboleda, it's also definitely worth making the drive up to **Siurana** (1) which is a spectacular village perched out on a sheer cliff at an altitude of over 700 meters with no guardrails around the edges. On clear days, the views are stunning and the village is also quite historic as it was the last bastion of Islam in Catalonia to be re-conquered by Christian forces in the 12th century.

"Barranc de la Bruixa" is technically in La Morera del Montsant, but it's included here due to being closer to Poboleda. There are three wineries located down the rather bumpy road that leads to this area which translates as "Witch's Gorge" in English. While it's possible to arrive there from Poboleda, the condition of those roads can be questionable and most anyone visiting this area should play it safe and come from the road that goes in the direction of Cornudella. It's a left hand turn just where the straight stretch of the road starts to bend coming from Venta del Pubill, the almighty regional landmark.

Suggested Itinerary
Start out first thing in the morning, with the early sun to visit **Mas Sinén**. If time permits, fit in a visit to **Genium** in the center of town, or **Hidalgo Albert** on the road towards Escaladei. Enjoy the lunch menu at **El Cau**, or if it's closed, head across the road to the **Casal la Closa**. If visiting on a weekend, stop in at the shop of **Agrícola de Poboleda** where they sell their wines as well as local products.

Finish up the day with a visit to **Mas Doix** and the stunning view from their old vineyards. Alternatively, if you're heading back towards Porrera or Falset in the evening, visit **Mas d'en Blei**.

Contacts

Cal Carles
977827267
Major, 19
Poboleda
www.calcarles.com

Càmping Poboleda
977827197
Plaça de les Casetes
Poboleda
www.campingpoboleda.net

Casal la Closa
Poboleda

El Cau
977827267
Carretera
Poboleda

Els Cups/ Hotel Populetus
977827045, 671049721
Raval, 16
Poboleda
www.populetus.com

Porta del Priorat
977821005
Carrertera de Poboleda
Cornudella

Venta del Pubill
Carretera Porrera-Cornudella, km 4
Cornudella

Approaching Poboleda from Escaladei

WINERIES

1. Marco Abella
2. Encastell
3. Ardèvol
4. Vall Llach
5. Joan Simó
6. Cal Pla
7. Clos Dominic
8. Balmaprat
9. Parmi
10. Castellet
11. Domaines Magrez
12. Sangenís i Vaqué
13. Cims de Porrera
14. Merum Priorati
15. Ferrer Bobet

WINE SHOPS

1. Vinum

SITES

1. Ruta dels Rellotges del Sol
2. The Old Bridge

AMENITIES

1. Café Priorat
2. Lo Teatret
3. Café Antic
4. La Cooperativa
5. Cal Carlets
6. Cal Porrerà
7. Mas Ardèvol
8. Hotel els Pàmpols
9. Mas d'en Gregori

- Municipality
- River
- Road
- Secondary road
- Wineries
- Sites
- Amenities
- Wine Shops

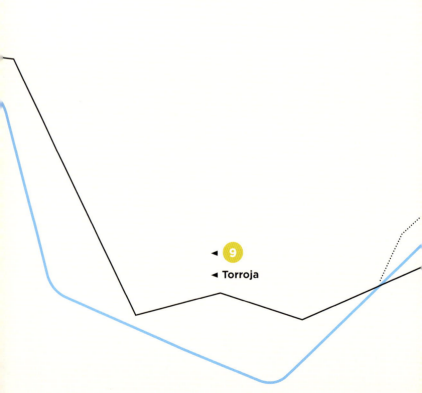

Porrera

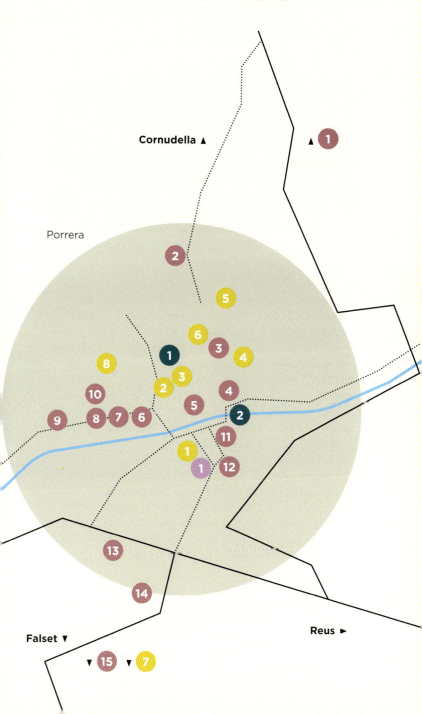

Porrera

With a population of about 500 people, Porrera is one of the larger villages in Priorat. Its name has two possible origins. One is that it came from the old Roman name found on documents from the 12th century (it gained a full town charter in 1201) of *"Valporriera"* which means "the valley of leeks". The other history of the name that locals like to tell is that it's a portmanteau of *"por"* meaning "fear" and *"enrera"* meaning "behind" which signified that the people moving in to this shady, "scary" valley full of wolves were finally leaving their fear behind them.

The village has also been at the crossroads of many historic battles including a dispute between two priories, the War of Succession, and the Napoleonic Wars. It was heavily fortified in the 13th century and remained so until the 18th century when the town walls and castle up on the hill above town were demolished.

In general, it's quite lively compared to the rest of the comarca which is due in no small part to its being just slightly closer to Barcelona than the other villages, so countless weekenders visit it. Obviously, the 15 wineries in town don't hurt either. While there's not much of the castle to see save for a few stones of the foundation, there is the **Ruta dels Rellotges del Sol** (1) which is a walking route around town to see their old sundials and of course there's the **Old Bridge** (2) which serves as a main crossing point over the Cortiella River that flows through the middle of the village.

Food options span a wide breadth with the basic, but filling fixed price lunches at **Café Priorat** (1) and **Café Antic** (3) to the more upscale dining of **Lo Teatret** (2), **La Cooperativa** (4), and **Cal Carlets** (5). Café Antic is noteworthy less for the dishes, but more for it being a village institution and everyone's meeting point. Famed Catalan poet Miquel Marti i Pol who spent two years in Porrera even wrote a poem about the café that is now painted on the wall. La Cooperativa is definitely the most sophisticated dining option and has the best wine list but it also has a very limited schedule due to catering mostly to weekend visitors.

The lodging offer is also quite good with **Cal Porrerà** (6) and **Hotel Els Pàmpols** (8) in the village and **Mas Ardèvol** (7) and **Mas d'en Gregori** (9) providing secluded, casa rural options outside of town. Mas Ardèvol organizes monthly dinners with local winemakers, so check their website to find out the details.

For those looking to purchase local wines, **Vinum** (1) is located on Plaça Catalunya aka "Friendly Village Cat Square" and as of 2013 is under new ownership with a new approach to local wine sales.

Suggested Itinerary

Start the day with a visit to **Marco Abella** just outside of town on the road to Cornudella. If there's time, fit in a visit to **Vall Llach**, **Cal Pla**, **Balmaprat**, or **Sangenís i Vaqué**. Depending on the day and budget, have lunch at either **La Cooperativa** or **Café Priorat**. In the afternoon, visit **Clos Dominic** and if there's time, **Ferrer Bobet**. Make sure to leave time for the early evening "vermut" at **Café Antic**.

Contacts

Café Antic
977828161
Onze de Setembre, 4
Porrera

Café Priorat
977828268
Plaça Catalunya, 1
Porrera

Cal Carlets
977828268
Secares, 5
Porrera

Cal Porrerà
977828310 | 620038175
Escoles, 4
Porrera
www.calporrera.com

La Cooperativa
977828378
Unió, 7
Porrera
www.restaurantlacooperativa.com

Hotel Els Pàmpols
977828382, 646610553
Obac, 1
Porrera
www.elspampols.net

Mas Ardèvol
977262270, 630324578
Carretera Falset-Porrera, km 5,3
Falset
www.masardevol.net

Mas d'en Gregori
977262297, 609732873
Carretera Porrera-Torroja, km 3,5
Porrera

Lo Teatret
977828195
Onze de Setembre, 4
Porrera

Cat comfort

WINERIES

1. Gratavinum
2. Buil & Giné
3. Mas Igneus
4. Trossos del Priorat
5. Ripoll Sans
6. B.G
7. Costers del Ros
8. Devinssi
9. Cesca Vicent
10. Masdéu i Campos
11. Cecilio
12. Balaguer i Cabré
13. Saó del Coster
14. Arrels del Priorat
15. Clos Erasmus
16. Vinícola del Priorat
17. Clos Figueras
18. Clos Mogador
19. Clos de l'Obac
20. Álavaro Palacios
21. Isabel Escanes Fuentes
22. Puig Priorat
23. Mas Martinet

SITES

1. Ermita de la Consolació

AMENITIES

1. La Font
2. Cal Llop
3. El Piró
4. El Forn del Pi
5. Cellers de Gratallops
6. Cal Llens
7. Hostal Elvira
8. La Cassola

WINE SHOPS

1. BonVlure
2. Agrobotiga

- Municipality
- River
- Road
- Secondary road
- Wineries
- Sites
- Amenities
- Wine Shops

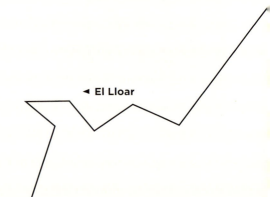

Gratallops

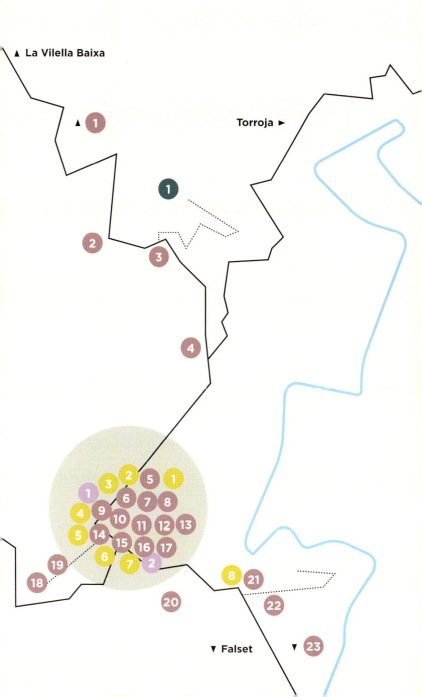

Gratallops

As a center of winemaking for Priorat and where the original Big Five founded their wineries, the village of Gratallops is host to no less than 23 wineries and many "flying winemakers" who use their cellars. It also is something of a crossroads and visitors will find themselves passing through this old village often. It received its town charter in 1258, although the village had been in existence long before that. It's seen ups and downs over the years, but ever since the 18th century, it has seen heavy cultivation of grapes, olives, and almonds.

The name is curious as in Catalan, it literally means, "scratching wolves" but there are theories that suggest due to some linguistic shifts over the centuries, it originally meant, "the place where wolves howl". This would be fitting given its perch up on the top of hill with the Siurana River trickling away down below and the hills coming up to it, endlessly slathered in terraced vineyards.

Above the village sits the **Ermita Mare de Déu de la Consolació** (1), a small hermitage that's still occupied these days with the nun-in-residence being quite knowledgeable on local hiking and flora. Apparently, you might even see her out jogging while wearing her habit. But, this small little stone building and the hill it is on are quite iconic and various wines from the village take their name from it or use it on their labels.

The food options in Gratallops are more plentiful than in other villages with places like the local butcher, **Cal Llens** (6) offering sandwiches for a couple of euros to the basic and filling **La Cassola** (8) just as you enter town, to the slightly more upscale **La Font** (1), **Cal Llop** (2), **El Piró** (3), **Les Figueres** at Clos Figueres, and **Cellers de Gratallops** (5). Cal Llop and La Font also have rooms to rent with the former being a fantastically decorated boutique hotel in an old, renovated farm house. For the more budget oriented, there is **Hostal Elvira** (7) next to the Agrobotiga of Vinícola del Priorat.

For buying wines, there are two great options in town at **BonVlure** (1) which is owned by the same people as El Piró and then there is the **Agrobotiga** (2) which has a very large selection of the wines from Gratallops and Priorat, and also sells meats, cheeses, and the incredible **DOP Siurana olive oil** they make at the cooperative as well as a few others. If you find that you're in need of some basic groceries or bread, stop in at **El Forn del Pi** (4) to stock up or visit **Mel de Gratallops** across the street for delicious local honey from the husband of the baker. Also interesting to take note of are the ceramics of **Ceramica del Priorat** made locally in the village and sold in their shop on the church square.

Suggested Itinerary

With so many great wineries, there are countless combinations to make for a memorable day spent in Gratallops. Start out in the morning with a visit to **Clos Mogador**, which includes a tour of their iconic vineyards. If there's time, fit in **Ripoll Sans** or **Cecilio**. Have lunch at either **El Piró** or **Cellers de Gratallops** across the street. If you have spare time at any point, drop in to **Buil & Giné** or **Cecilio** who readily accommodate walk-in tastings. In the afternoon, try to visit either **Clos de l'Obac** or **Saó de Coster**. In the later afternoon, go for a tasting at **Trossos del Priorat**, then have a "vermut" at **Cal Llop**. Stay there for dinner, or try the Clos Figueras restaurant, **Les Figueres**. Again, there are many variations to try and these are just suggested starting points.

Contacts

Cal Llens
La Font, 38
Gratallops

La Font
977839279
Consolació, 12
Gratallops

Cal Llop/La Boca del Llop
977839502
De dalt, 21
Gratallops
www.cal-llop.com

La Cassola
977262146
Carretera Falset-Gratallops, km 8.5
Gratallops

Cellers de Gratallops
977839036
Piró, 32
Gratallops

Ceramica del Priorat
977839017
Plaça Eglesia
Gratallops

La Font
977839279
Consolació, 12
Gratallops

El Forn del Pi
977839269
Piró, 40
Gratallops

Hostal Elvira
977839167
Piró, 43
Gratallops
www.hostalelvira.com

El Piró/Vinateria Bon Vlure
977839004, 977839130
Piró, 21
Gratallops

Les Figueres
977830217
La Font, 38
Gratallops
www.lesfigueres.com

Lunch at El Piró

WINERIES

1. Torres Priorat
2. Prior Pons
3. Clos 93
4. Agnès de Cervera
5. Mas Garrian
6. Clos del Portal
7. La Perla del Priorat
8. De Muller
9. Morlanda
10. Pins Vers
11. Domini de la Cartoixa
12. Clos Berenguer

SITES

1. Coves dels Rogerals

AMENITIES

1. Perxe

- Municipality
- River
- Road
- Secondary Road
- Wineries
- Sites
- Amenities
- Level River Crossing

El Lloar, El Molar

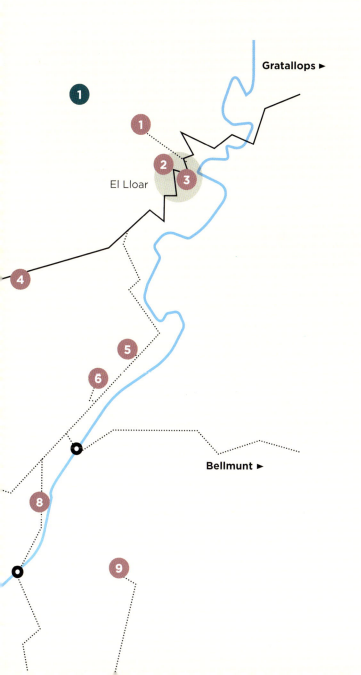

El Lloar

Lloar-Molar

El Lloar

A small village just to the west of Gratallops, El Lloar's name either has an Arabic root meaning, "the slopes" or a Latin root meaning, "abundant flat stones/slate". Either name is fitting as it is perched out on a hill with a great deal of the llicorella to be found around it. Existing with its current name since the 17th century (albeit spelled as El Lloá, which is how Lloar is pronounced) the village is the smallest in Priorat at just over 100 residents. The most dominant part of it is the Torres winery, although others are sprouting up as well.

For those interested in doing a little hike, there's a trail that heads out from the north side of El Lloar by the Torres winery and continues all the way to the village of La Figuera that offers great views of the valley. Just 2km in to the trail there are caves carved into the red rocks that are called, **Coves dels Rogerals** (1).

El Molar

Old ruins dating from 600BC are very close to el Molar and show the founding of the village to be from antiquity with a Roman origin. The name is thought to be derived from the word for "mill" and referred to those that were historically in the area, constructed from the red sandstone that's abundant up in the Montsant cliffs.

Serving as a crossroads for the area to other villages, it was part of the neighboring Garcia municipality until the mid 19th century. These days, the 300 or so residents make a living the same way as they have for generations via wine, oil, and almonds. For those looking to stay in El Molar, **Perxe** (1) offers a casa rural with space for up to 12 people and the option to stay with a different Catalan writer in residence each month.

Siurana River Crossings One goes in the direction of Bellmunt and the other to el Masroig. While not deep at all and designed for a passenger car to easily drive across, the water volume can be increased upstream and the unwary can find their car swept off the concrete crossing point. Listen to announcements or ask locals about the river status, especially when there is rain.

Suggested Itinerary

Start the morning with a visit to **Torres Priorat**. If there's time, try to make a visit with **Clos 93**. Go back up the road to Gratallops and have lunch at **Cellers de Gratallops**. In the afternoon, stop by **Agnès de Cervera** and/or **La Perla de Priorat**.

Contacts

Perxe
977825504, 670544420
De la Font
El Molar

WINERIES

1. Gran Clos
2. Bartolomé
3. Solà Clàssic
4. Casa Gran del Siurana
5. Sedó Barceló
6. Mas d'en Gil
7. Pinord Mas Blanc
8. Capafons-Ossó
9. William David Garsed

WINE SHOPS

1. Vinateria Aguiló
2. Vins i olis del Priorat

SITES

1. Museu de les Mines
2. Castell del Vi
3. Hermita de Sant Gregori

AMENITIES

1. Hostal Sport
2. El Cairat
3. Entrepà i Pa
4. Quinoa
5. El Celler de l'Àspic
6. Calaix de Sastre
7. Marçà-Falset Train Station
8. L'Economat de les Mines

- Municipality
- Highway
- River
- Road
- Secondary road
- Wineries
- Sites
- Amenities
- Wine Shops

Gratallops ▲

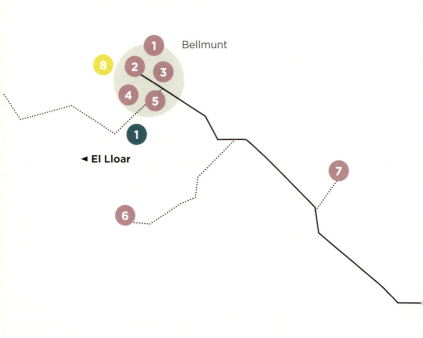

Bellmunt, Falset

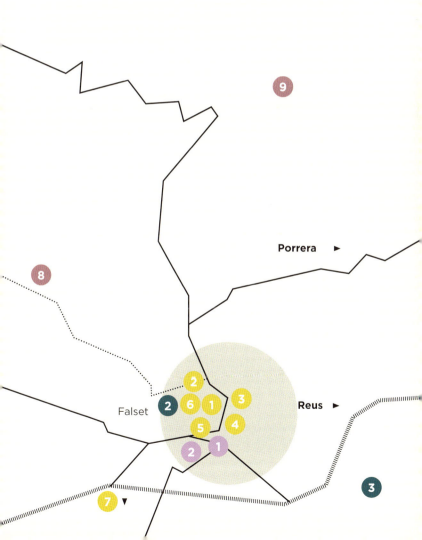

Bellmunt del Priorat

Bellmunt-Falset

Bellmunt del Priorat
What put Bellmunt on the map was its mines. The Romans were aware of the mineral riches in the village and happily dug in to the hills thousands of years ago. The use of the mines only increased with industrialization to the point where they closed down in 1972 due to rising costs of extracting their main mineral, lead ore. The mining industry left an imprint on this village with old company barracks taking up the town, as well as mining buildings.

Those interested in the history of the mines, should visit the **Museu de les Mines** (1) which is open weekends. If looking for a place to eat while checking out the mines and wines, stop at **L'Economat de les Mines** (8) which has one of the most affordable and diverse dinner menus with traditional dishes to be found in Priorat.

Falset
While a portion of Falset's town limits are within DOQ Priorat, the town itself is in neighboring DO Montsant. But, being the largest town in the area with the county seat,

many amenities, and one of only two gas stations in all of Priorat (the other being in Cornudella del Montsant), visitors will undoubtedly pass through it a great deal.

The generally accepted origin of the name is from the Catalan word for *"sickle"* and a pair of them even adorns the town's shield, although some claim the name has an Arabic root. While this debate will probably never be solved, the origins of this town easily date back to the Prehistoric Era.

Throughout the centuries, Falset found itself as a focal point for a great many battles. The Medieval castle that still exists on the main hill of the town can still be seen today, but was in a state of ruin just a few years ago due to the Napoleonic Wars in the early 19th century. The entire structure was recently restored and now houses **Castell del Vi** (2), a wine museum for the area with a tasting area and frequent events, albeit with sporadic opening hours. Also interesting is the **Ermita de Sant Gregori** (3) which is on the other side of the main road in to Falset. Dug out of a sandstone cliff, it's especially impressive at sunset.

For lodging and food options, **Hostal Sport** (1) is the best overall choice. A hotel that's been a family business for several generations, the current family member running it, Marta Domènech can help visitors make appointments to visit the wineries and is a fount of information about Priorat. In spite of being the largest hotel in the region with 18 rooms, it's still quite intimate and has a very convenient café that seems to be always open as well as a great restaurant serving tasty local specialties.

For general, basic eating, **Entrepà i Pa** (3) across from Hostal Sport offers simple sandwiches at a good price for the budget minded. The restaurants, **El Cairat** (2), **Quinoa** (4), and **El Celler de l'Àspic** (5) offer the best higher end options to be found, although the service at Quinoa leaves much to be desired. El Celler de l'Àspic is especially noteworthy for its extensive local and international (ie French) wine list and the owner's extensive knowledge about wine, as well as exquisitely crafted modern cuisine. And for a great wine bar showing off the region, stop in at **Calaix de Sastre** (6)

The two wines shops in Falset, **Vinateria Aguiló** (1) and **Vins i Olis del Priorat** (2) do the job of bringing the entire offer of wines to one spot. Almost every bottle made in the region can be found at either of these shops and at overall competitive prices, especially when compared to buying outside the region.

For those arriving by train, the **Marçà-Falset station** (7) is located about 2.2km southwest from the center of town making for an easy bike ride or a longer, but doable walk.

Suggested Itinerary

Plan the full morning around a visit to **Capafons-Ossó**. Pencil in time to have a "vermut" (yes it's not just for before dinner) at **Hostal Sport** in Falset. Have lunch there or at one of the other restaurants in town. In the afternoon, visit **Pinord's Mas Blanc** or **Solà Classic**. Have a coffee in between visits at **L'Economat de les Mines**.

Contacts

Museu de les Mines
626384706, 977830578
Carretera de la Mina
Bellmunt

www.minesbellmunt.com

L'Economat de les Mines
977831346, 669892766
Clos, 10
Bellmunt

www.leconomatdelesmines.com

El Cairat
977830481, 620928618
Nou, 3
Falset
www.restaurantelcairat.com

El Celler de l'Àspic
977831246
Miquel Barceló, 31
Falset
www.cellerdelaspic.com

Entrepà i Pa
977830294
Catalunya, 6
Falset

Quinoa
977830431
Miquel Barceló, 29
Falset
www.restaurantquinoa.com

Hostal Sport
977830078
Miquel Barceló, 4
Falset
www.hotelpriorat-hostalsport.com

Calaix de Sastre
687814144
Plaça de la Quartera, 39
Falset

Vinateria Aguiló
977830776
Miquel Barceló, 11
Falset
www.aguilo-prioratwines.com

Vins i Olis del Priorat
977831835
Miquel Barceló, 25
Falset
www.vinsiolisdelpriorat.com

Banquet hall at Hostal Sport

Cellers

 104

 315

Antoni Basté Garriga, due to his friendship with René Barbier, made wine in Priorat for the first time in 1989 with the initial group of people who started a new "revolution". But he ended up selling his share to the other partners. Then in 2001-2002 his enolog sons Julià and Jeroni started working again in the region, at the Laurona winery in DO Montstant. Shortly after they all decided to restart making wine in Priorat and so between 2003 and 2007 they organized a 10 hectare property where they planted local varietals as well as trying other unusual ones like Roussane and Tannat.

Jeroni made his first wine, Alice, in 2004. Although his wines are produced solely from his vineyards in Gratallops, in the eight years since the first vintage he's found himself using various different cellars in Gratallops. But he's now looking to settle down and working with local architect Joan Farreras (who also happens to make a wine named, Clos de l'Ona) to rehabilitate an old house in the village that will be the final home for the Abadia winery. These days he makes eight different wines: Alice, six different Sant Jeroni, and Clos Clara.

Jeroni Basté Wittig
owner & enolog

GPS
41.176599
0.730032

Celler de L'Abadia
Gratallops, *Carrer de l'Era, 5*

Visits: Not currently open for public visits
Contact: 627032134 | jeroni@cellerabadia.com
Website: www.cellerabadia.com
Languages: English, French

Sant Jeroni 2010 opens with a bit of pear to the nose and a great deal of mineral character. In the body, it shows off a well built acidity that's refreshing while also substantial. A touch of lemon peel character comes up and it begs to be paired with a meal.
70% Pedro Ximénez, 30% Carignan/Grenache/Viognier

● | 13,5% | 16-18€ |

Alice 2007 takes its name from Jeroni's sister. It has a nose that's initially loaded with dark fruits along with a touch of sweetness and oak at the bottom of it. Full on the palate, it flows with plush aspects in the texture. The acidity starts out rather strong but as it opens up, the wine softens a great deal.
Syrah, Mourvèdre, Grenache, Carignan, Cab Sauvignon

● | 13,5% | 20-24€ |

GPS
41.176599
0.730032

Agnès de Cevera
El Molar, *Carretera El Molar-El Lloar, km.10*

Visits: Regular tours including a visit to the winery, their vineyards and a guided tasting of two of their wines are offered daily during their opening hours for 9€ a person. It's best to call ahead for a reservation.
Contact: 977054851, 618104140 | comunicacion@agnesdecervera.com
Website: www.agnesdecervera.com
Languages: English

In between El Molar and El Lloar, there are heavy, scruffy patches of pine trees that make you feel as if you're driving in to a forested region of Priorat. But, for a brief stretch, the trees part and the terraced vineyards of Agnès de Cervera spill down the hills and wrap around their modern winery.

Initially they started in 2003 in a rented cellar up in the village of Porrera where they have 20 hectares of vineyards. It happened that the chance arose in 2010 to buy this cellar in El Molar from the original owner (the very large Osborne Company) who had built it just a few years earlier. The name of the winery is a combination of the owner's granddaughter's name and his grandmother's last name.

It all seems to have fit them well as they now harvest from a total of 32 hectares, of which they own 85%. These vineyards happily grow in Porrera as well as the area surrounding their winery. Annually they're producing around 75,000 bottles and this new winery allows them to easily hold their 150 barrels of mostly French oak in a rather stunning underground cellar. Their enolog is Fran Vernet.

It should also be noted that they produce their own olive oil from the Arbequina trees in their property. Like many other oils in Priorat, it is full-bodied and has expressive aromas and is wonderfully buttery in texture.

Barrel cellar

La Petite Agnès 2011 is a young wine that they created as an introductory label that manages to have a deep nose with larger sweet components and hints of dusty spices. The body isn't as luxurious as their aged wines, but still has a great deal of depth and character for a young wine with red fruits and light acidity that would pair well with meals.
85% Grenache, 10% Carignan, 10% Cab Sauvignon

● | 14,5% | 5.90-7€ | ⚖

Argeles 2008 has bright red fruits and an underlying aspect of minerality to the nose which changes considerably with just a little decanting to put out dark fruits and elements of figs. The nose translates well in to the body with a boost of acidity that pulls through in to the finish. It's a generally pleasant mix of elements in the body that all play well together.
85% Grenache, 15% Carignan

● | 14,5% | 10.50-12€ | ⚖

Lytos 2010 has a darker, spicier nose with dark fruits. The body is relatively plush with a slight hint of bitterness and touches of leather that come through in the finish. Larger in the mouth, it fills out the palate and presents a bolder glass of wine that could be sipped at a bar for hours. Hazelnuts and caramel grow in the nose as it breathes.
45% Carignan, 35% Grenache, 15% Syrah, 5% Cab Sauvignon

● | 15% | 16.50-20€ | ⚖ | ✸

Kalos 2009 is made from their 85 year-old vines. The nose picks up a strong violet aspect from the old Carignan and presents an overall floral composition. As it breathes, pepper elements come out as well. In the body, it maintains its freshness, but is quite concentrated, eventually allowing some cocoa to emerge with time as well as refined minerality that carries in to the finish.
50% Carignan, 35% Syrah, 15% Cab Sauvignon

● | 15% | 20-25€

Jordi Puxeu
manager & enolog

GPS
41.235061
0.846199

Agrícola de Poboleda
Poboleda, *Carrer Portal*

Visits: While not generally open for public visits, they do have a small shop at the level of the road which is open weekends and holidays for people looking to purchase their wines directly. Like most shops in the area, they also have a number of local products that are definitely worth checking out.
Contact: 977827004 | agricolapoboleda@gmail.com
Website: www.cellcr3unio.com

Inviting, is perhaps not the first word that comes to mind when standing outside this winery which sits alongside the main road through Poboleda. Built in 1954, its large blocky concrete walls don't encourage one to want to venture inside. Of course what happens behind the walls of this fortress of wine is something of a different story. After 12 years of being a mix of a private winery and a cooperative, in 2004 they became part of the Cellers Unió group and underwent a full remodel and restructuring to modernize their production. They now have the potential capacity to produce over half a million liters of wine a year.

Spread over multiple levels are the large stainless steel tanks and barrels lodged amongst the old concrete aging tanks that they converted to barrel aging rooms in 2004. Deftly working through all of this, manager and enolog, Jordi Puxeu crafts the blends of grapes from the 33 members of the cooperative. They still use four of their old concrete tanks, as well as stainless-steel tanks. For long term aging they have a unique 50/50 split of French and American oak barrels of which about 30% are used barrels from previous vintages.

These days they focus their production on Grenache and Carignan with smaller amounts of other varieties, and make three different lines of wines: Llicorella, Tendral, and Enuc–this last one made specifically for supermarkets.

Barrel aging cellar

Roureda Llicorella Blanc Únic 2010 starts out with smokiness on top of the core minerality in the aromas. It has a surprisingly light body with small citric notes and white fruits. The acidity picks up in the finish, but the wine stay refreshing overall. As it breathes, all these rather disparate elements come together in a pleasing equilibrium.

100% Pedro Ximénez

 | 14%

Tendral Selecció 2009 shows off the dark fruits in its nose well, while tossing in a good dose of graphite minerality. It's plush with large fruit on the palate as well as juicy and meaty all the way in to the finish. The finish is slightly dry and raises a small degree of acidity on the way out.

Grenache, Carignan

 | 14.5%

Llicorella Gran Seleccićo 2006 has a buttery and soft nose with a touch of anise and minerality that comes up. The body carries the butter, but picks up more tannins and acidity, while keeping a good balance of all aspects. The finish is quick and light with slight red fruit tartness before it closes.

Grenache, Carignan, Cab Sauvignon, Syrah

 | 14.5%

Roureda Llicorella Negre 2005 has a warm, mineral nose with a mix of red and dark fruits. Beeswax, waffle, and spicy red fruit are the most prominent flavors in the body as well as dry, big acids. The finish has the acids lingering in to it and with air, the wine gets larger overall.

Grenache, Carignan, Cab Sauv, Merlot, Tempranillo

 | 14.5%

Jordi Aixalà
owner

GPS
41.213989
0.809925

Aixalà Alcait
Torroja del Priorat, *Carrer de Balandra, 8*

Visits: They have tastings and tours of their cellars for free with purchase, otherwise the price is 5€ per person. Call ahead to reserve a time.
Contact: 977839516,629507807 | pardelasses@gmail.com
Website: www.pardelasses.com
Languages: English, German

If visitors to Torroja del Priorat are completely charmed by the village, and it's hard not to be, then it's worth noting that Jordi Aixalà has been the mayor of this small village for the past decade. More recently, he's also been the Aixalà part of the name of this winery (the other name, Alcait being his wife Susi's family name). Affable and incredibly friendly, it's easy to see why he has managed to do well in politics, as well as in wine with all of his bottles seeming to carry the jovial, yet serious spirit that pervades their maker.

Although in 1994 they took over the vineyards that had been in the family for generations, they're a relatively new winery as they had their first vintage in 2005 with just 2,200 bottles produced. Since then, they've been growing steadily and even managed to outgrow their original cellar in the bottom of Jordi's mother's home. They've constructed a new cellar a short distance away (it is a tiny village after all) with larger production capabilities and also the ability to host visitors with greater ease. Visitors taste their wines with a westerly view out over the mountains that surround the small valley in which Torroja calls home.

They're currently harvesting from 17.5 hectares which they've been farming organically since 2011 and they age their wines in a mix of 300 and 500L barrels, drifting more to the larger ones with time as they, like many in Priorat are working to have less pronounced oak aspects in their wines.

Cellar tasting terrace

Destrankis 2011 opens up warm on the nose. It shows its time spent in the oak as dark berry aromas come in and out of play. In the body, it fills out the palate and is overall very meaty but manages to maintain a good balance of characteristics that carry in to the finish.

80% Carignan, 20% Grenache

 ● | 14,5% | 12-13€

Pardelasses 2011 is quite potent and strong right out of the bottle, presenting dark, jammy berries in the nose. The body has leathery aspects and strong tannins, with a pleasant, fleshy quality. Given time, it does mellow somewhat, but is still quite large and would be best had with roasted meats and spicy dishes.

50% Grenache, 50% Carignan

● | 15% | 15-16€

Les Clivelles de Torroja 2010 tosses out strong red and black fruits that then drift in to mineral elements, with a slight almond quality at the fringes. The body changes to spicy, herbaceous flavors and while concentrated, it still has a great deal of character.

100% Carignan

● | 14% | 15€ | ⚖ | ✹

Coster de l'Alzina 2011 is the Catalan name for the cork oak tree as well as Jordi and Susi's daughter. It spends 12 months in 500L barrels. The nose is of leather and light hints of tobacco. It's initially smooth across the palate, but shows a rather understated minerality that gives way to the herbal elements and a decent amount of acidity arrives in the finish. As it decants, it smoothes quickly and shows off its overall equilibrium. Roasted root vegetables and earthiness come in to the nose as well as chewiness to the back taste of the finish.

100% Carignan

● | 14% | 25€

AIXALÀ ALCAIT

Álvaro Palacios
owner & enolog

GPS
41.190031
0.779985

Álvaro Palacios

Gratallops, *Carretera Gratallops-Falset, km 0.4*

Visits: Not currently open for public visits
Contact: 977839195 | info@alvaropalacios.com

Situated across the road from the village of Gratallops, the sleek, modern, and unsigned winery of Álvaro Palacios has a commanding view of the region. The youngest member of the original group who came to Priorat in the late 1980s to revitalize the wine scene in Priorat, Álvaro and his wines have gained some of the biggest buzz and, as seen with L'Ermita, the biggest prices.

Álvaro wasn't a newcomer to wine when he started down this road. His family had been making wine in Rioja for some 150 years and he was born in their home right above the cellar. The second youngest of nine children, growing up he wanted to be a matador but instead he went to France to study enology and learn the craft in Bordeaux. He also worked a few harvests in world renowned wineries such as Château Petrus in Pomerol and Stag's Leap in Napa Valley.

Upon returning to Spain, he primarily worked as a wine barrel salesman until he learned that René Barbier III (who was working for Álvaro's family in Rioja) was heading to Priorat to start a new wine venture. He ran off with next to no money and worked to start his own winery from scratch alongside René and the others, releasing an initial vintage with the rest of the group in 1989. He continued in a small cellar in the middle of Gratallops, and in 1998 moved to his gorgeous winery up on a hill designed by architect Jesús Manzanares.

In 1993 he bought a small plot next to the Consolació hermitage with 1.3 hectares of Grenache vines planted in 1939 and 0.2 planted in 1910. With them he started making his cult wine "L'Ermita", initially blended with Cabernet and since 2006 almost only Grenache. From there everything grew in leaps and bounds over the decades to the point where his winery now has 40ha of vineyards, 26 of which are certified organic and out of those 10 are in steep slopes that require plowing using the traditional method by mule.

Álvaro has been a constant champion for Priorat throughout the decades. In 2007 he worked with the DOQ body to establish the "Vi de la vila" certification in an effort to further show the remarkable soil and grapes that come from Priorat. A strong proponent of Grenache in the region, he's gone so far as to cut back his old Cabernet Sauvignon vines and re-graft new Grenache vines on them after noting that the latter grape is a better fit for Priorat. He's now a strong Grenache proponent and is very passionate with the results it produces.

This focus, passion, and Álvaro's general charm have all proven to be good for business as they export to 70 countries now and from the depths of their impressive barrel aging cellar an annual production of 330,000 bottles emerges. The famous L'Ermita is but a small drop of that, with just 1,300 bottles per vintage that sit off to one side in lone two barrels, waiting for a devoted public that can't seem to get enough of it.

Their terraced vineyards

The l'Ermita aging

Camins del Priorat 2011 has slight hints of violets mixed in with a little licorice, rich red fruits and just a tinge of boysenberry. It's light in the mouth and has a dry, well structured build of acids and general freshness overall. It's a wine best suited for all around drinking or meal pairing.
40% Carignan, 30% Grenache, 30% Cab Sauvignon/Syrah/Merlot

 | 14,5% | 14,50€

Les Terrasses 2011 shows off darker fruits with an underlying creamy caramel component to the nose that changes a bit in to slightly smoky aspect with time. Round and bright in the mouth, it tosses about its minerality with a great deal of fun. It floats about on the palate quite lightly. Tannins are present but not potent. The finish is quick, clean, and easygoing with a hint of leather picking up as it breathes. A dusty cocoa aspect comes up while the acidity backs off a bit.
50% Grenache, 45% Carignan, 5% Cab Sauv/Syrah

● | 14,5% | 25€

Gratallops 2011 is a fully estate wine. The nose presents itself fully and proudly, fluffing up the nostrils as you inhale it. A touch spicy, buts smooth overall and it lets a lot of the local herb aromas come through. The minerality appears immediately, but in a different way as if drinking from a fresh mineral spring. It maintains a very delicate balance as it breathes. The body continues with this natural, earthy quality, but isn't the least bit heavy which translates in to this fleeting, wonderful finish that leaves with just a touch of herbs on the palate.

70% Grenache, 30% Carignan

● | 14,5% | 40€ |

Finca Dolfí 2011 puts out aromas of orange peel, herbs, and a touch of prune. It's wickedly twisty in the nose and keeps shifting the aromas as it breathes. Soft in the mouth, the tannins come through more, but still, the acidity is held in a very smart balance with the other aspects. Chocolate and very small coffee elements stick in the corners of the palate and drift in to the finish that lingers with the acids. As it breathes, the texture dries out a bit and loses some of the initially plush tannins. Overall it shows itself off as a super complex and deep wine.

95% Grenache, 5% Carignan/Syrah

● | 14,5% | 65€ |

L'Ermita 2009 is the ultimate wine from Priorat both in reputation and in price. It sees an extremely small release of just 1,300 bottles per year. It is made with the utmost care and craft in the winery with just two 500L barrels off to one side holding the entire biodynamic production for the year. Swooned over by critics year after year, it constantly remains an elusive bottle despite the price.

Grenache, Carignan, White Grenache, Macabeu

● | 14,5% | 850€

ÁLVARO PALACIOS

Josep and Albert Ardèvol are originally from Porrera and like many families in the village they've held on to family vines that were tended by grandparents, great-grandparents, and probably even further up the branches in the family tree. Up until the late 1990s, they were selling off their high-quality grapes to other wineries, including Mas Martinet. In 2000 they started up their own cellar and partnering with Roser Galceran, they initially produced 5,600 bottles.

As the years have passed, they now produce about 35,000 bottles produced from 10 hectares of vineyards spread over three properties, and use the services of popular enolog consultant, Roser Amorós to take care of the winemaking.

They have a modern cellar with the typical stainless steel tanks you see in similar wineries in the region, except the grapes aging there are passionately guarded by two lovable hounds. Then, there is the fascinating old family cellar where the barrel aging takes place. Located in one of the most picturesque old homes in Porrera, the barrels sit about a basement draped with vaulted stone ceilings. Carved in to the rock, it's a striking setting.

Josep Ardèvol
owner

GPS
41.188757
0.856601

Ardèvol i Associats

Porrera, *Carrer Barceloneta, 14*

Visits: Not currently open for public visits
Contact: 977828057 | cellerardevol@yahoo.es
Website: www.cellerardevol.cat

Anjoli 2009 has rough mineral elements present at the core of it, but also presents unpleasantly high tannins and acidity across the top and makes for a tough glass to get in to and will be challenging to most people. Given lengthy decanting, some of the less desirable elements blow off.

Grenache, Carignan, Cab Sauvignon, Merlot, Syrah

● | 14,5% | 10-12€

Coma d'en Romeu 2009 is relatively plush on the palate with a good brace of tannins coming up as it decants that then linger in to the finish with a slight touch of tar and tobacco. While larger in the body than the Anjoli, it's a little rounder, allowing it to pair with meals and be generally more passable.

Cab Sauvignon, Merlot, Syrah, Grenache

● | 14,5% | 16-18€

Arrels, which means roots in Catalan, is one of the most interesting projects to be created in some time in Priorat. It's a romantic initiative by friends Jaume Balaguér of Celler Balaguer i Cabré and René Barbier of Clos Mogador to showcase a dying tradition in Priorat. For those unfamiliar with it, "vi ranci" is a traditional oxidized wine without added alcohol that, for as long as memory serves was made by Catalan families at home to sip slowly on special occasions or had with guests. Taking years to age properly in the solera system, it was never a wine that would commercialize easily despite being a Catalan "brandy".

Both being huge fans of vi ranci and feeling sad that the tradition was disappearing, Jaume and René set out in 1997 to find the best vi rancis in Priorat. They visited many old families in villages around the area to sample the different ones produced at home. From this research they found seven vi rancis that they bottled separately under the name of each house: Cal Batllet, Cal Boter and Cal Piró from Gratallops, Cal Pagès from Bellmunt, Cal Ferrando from Poboleda, Cal Sabaté from La Vilella Baixa and Ca les Viudes from Porrera. This last one has a 100 year-old mother and is an extremely rare vi ranci that is 140€ a bottle.

Jaume Balaguer
owner

Arrels del Priorat
Gratallops, *Carrer de Piró 83*

Visits: Not currently open for public visits
Contact: 977839171

Arrels 30 Anys is a complex, serious wine to be viewed at the level of a fine cognac. Aromas of apricots, figs, and quince are all found in the nose. The body is initially a touch acidic on the tip of the tongue but this gives way to how it lusciously coats the palate with hints of toasted almonds and walnuts.
100% Grenache

 | 20.2% | 25-30€

They also made a blend of different barrels using a 30 year-old mother that they called Arrels 30 Anys. These days, this is the only vi ranci that they continue to produce in their dedicated cellar with a production that ranges from 500 and 1,000 bottles a year. Finding traditional chestnut barrels too aggressive, they decided to introduce custom-made French oak barrels of different sizes. All things considered, this is a labor of love that at the end of the year yields just enough profit to buy a meal at the restaurant.

Jaume Balaguer
Roser Cabré
owners

GPS
41.192838
0.776523

Balaguer i Cabré
Gratallops, *Carrer de la Font, 8*

Visits: Available for 5€ a person on weekends and holidays, with prior booking two days in advance. They can also organize tastings paired with meals at the family restaurant Piró.
Contact: 977839004, 626175077, 650107954 | vins.jaume@yahoo.com
Website: cellerbalaguercabre.blogspot.com
Languages: English, French

Like many Priorat natives, Jaume Balaguer's family had been cultivating vines and making wine at home for generations. Unfortunately, they stopped and Jaume worked in other businesses in his youth. Then, some twenty years ago he decided, along with his wife Maria Pilar Cabré to recuperate the old vineyards and start making wine again. After a couple of "test" vintages they produced their first bottled wine in 2005, and are now making two different, single-estate monovarietal Grenache wines with a third on the way.

They believe Grenache is the varietal that can best tell the story of Priorat and over the years they realized that each vineyard had a markedly different character depending on the orientation and altitude so they decided to make separate wines. At the moment they are the only winery that focuses all their production on one varietal, showcasing so clearly the importance of the locale. While the "Big Five" brought a technological revolution to Priorat in the late 1970s and 1980s, there is now a second revolution of the terroir led by wineries like Balaguer i Cabré.

The family also owns one of the best restaurants in Priorat, Piró, and Jaume Balaguer Jr. runs the wine shop Bon VIure next door focusing only on wines from the Priorat comarca.

Jaume Balaguer Jr. in the cellar

Ruella 2010 shows off a lot of herbal elements to the nose including chamomile and thyme. The body has a sweeter aspect to it and is quite full of red fruits. All of this comes out in to a dry finish.

100% Grenache

● | 14,5% | 12-13€

La Guinardera 2008 starts out with a light, gentle nose showing just a touch of minerality to it. This picks up more in the body and the textures of the vineyards come through more. Light blackberry and red fruits develop, framing the lovely soft aspect of the body on the palate.

100% Grenache

● | 14,5% | 15-16€ | ✺

A tasting in their wine shop

A compact family cellar, Balmaprat produces a small run of 1,600 bottles a year from their half a hectare vineyard of mixed vines located just south of the village. Josep Maria del Águila and Mayte Pellicer are a couple who have long had a passion for wine, but it was in 2008 that they decided to start their winery with the help of Adrià Pérez of Cims de Porrera who is their enolog.

The main floor of their cellar is where all the production happens and is lined with their press, tanks, and other winemaking apparatuses. Below that is a nicely restored cellar where they keep their barrels, nestled in loose bits of the local llicorella stones to maintain humidity. They have a small area for tasting alongside various old amphorae and urns as well as the signature "water mine" at the back of it which so many cellars in Porrera lay claim to.

While currently releasing their main Dempeus wine, they are soon releasing a higher end Dempeus Seleció that showcases their 125 year-old, single vineyard Carignan grapes that they used to sell off to other wineries.

Josep M. del Águila
Mayte Pellicer
owners

GPS
41.188127
0.85516

Balmaprat

Porrera, *Carrer Prat de la Riba, 7*

Visits: There is no cost for visits, but they are conducted on a limited basis, so call ahead to reserve a time.
Contact: 649688073,606828145 | balmaprat@hotmail.com
Website: www.facebook.com/balmaprat

Dempeus 2008 sees 18 months of aging. The nose opens with aromas of plum and dark fruits that all transfer in to the body. It's a touch sweet across the palate and this aspect carries in to the finish to complete a well balanced wine.
30% Carignan, 25% Grenache, 25% Cab Sauvignon, 15% Merlot, 5% Syrah

🔴 | 14,5% | 14-16€ |

Dempeus Sel•lecció 2009 is a very unique, elegant Carignan made with 125 year-old vines. The nose is light but with a good dose of bitter chocolate that transfers in to mineral elements in the body. It's very fresh and approachable but still filled with great, old character. It's a very limited release wine with only 260 bottles a year.
100% Carignan

🔴 | 15% | 30-40€ |

Down the main road that loops through the village of Bellmunt, the cellar of Rosa Maria Bartolomé Vernet is an unassuming building, tucked off on the side. While they have had family vineyards for some time that are 80-110 years old, they were selling the grapes of these Carignan and Grenache vines to other wineries. These other wineries were fortunate to be buying such old grapes and a bit of history as their 110 year-old vineyard was the first one to be replanted in Bellmunt after the devastation of phylloxera.

Although they had been making wine in bulk at home for years, in 1998 they established their cellar and started bottling their own wines. Owners Rosa and Antonio have since been working to show what the grapes from their three properties (El Grinyó, Mas de Caldera, and Els Molins) are capable of by releasing both shorter and longer termed aged red wines. Typical years show them bottling 8-10,000 bottles, although in recent years production has been down for economic reasons including Priorat's difficult seasons for the last couple of years.

Rosa Bartolomé
owner

GPS
41.164519
0.766859

Bartolomé
Bellmunt del Priorat, *Carrer Major 23*

Visits: Saturdays are preferred for visits with a maximum of 10 people and a cost of 12€ per person.
Contact: 977320448,616478581 | cellerbartolome@hotmail.com
Website: www.primitiudebellmunt.com

Clos Bartolomé 2008 has an interesting, somewhat sweet nose to it. The body is more typical of the region wherein it has some depth and notes of chocolate but stops a bit short of full deepness. As such, it's a lighter wine that would be suited for meals.
50% Grenache, 40% Carignan, 10% Cab Sauvignon

● | 14,5% | 6€

Primitiu de Bellmunt 2005 shows a spicy, dark fruit nose that carries in to the body a good deal. The body brings up acidity as well as trace minerality that comes up a bit more as it decants with a touch of violet coming in to play. The finish is a touch dry, but carries out the herbal notes that develop in the wine.
60% Grenache 40% Carignan

● | 15% | 12€

Made in the cellars of Joan Simó, this is a personal project by Steve Colombé thanks to his friendship with Gerard Batllevell. Steve is an English fellow with training as a plant physiologist who has been coming down for the last decade to help out with the harvest. Starting in 2008, he worked out an exchange to make a couple of barrels with a selection of grapes from the Joan Simó vineyards to make his 585 bottles. In addition to his time in Priorat, he's also made four vintages of wines under the 'Domaine Pic Aubeil' name in the Roussillon region of France.

Each vintage of his wine sees Steve trying some different approaches such as with his latest one which he plans to age six months in the barrel followed by another 12 in a clay amphora.

The name of the wine in Catalan is a reference to the phrase "the cat's whiskers" meaning something at the height of perfection.

Steve Colombé
owner

Els Bigotis del Gat
Porrera

Visits: Not currently open for public visits
Contact: 633586500, +44 1363775973 | steve@picaubeil.co.uk

Els Bigotis del Gat 2010 sees 15 months in French oak. The nose is mineral and stony with touches of leather and an understated citric quality. Initially buttery and round in the mouth, the acidity comes up with a little air as well as a great deal of freshness. It's dry, but easy to drink and nicely balanced.
58% Carignan, 30% Syrah, 12% Cab Sauvignon

● | 15% | 20€

Using the facilities at Cecilio, where he also works as an enolog and is married to one of the daughters, Blai Ferré has been producing his own wine since 2007. In 1999 he planted vines on 6.5 hectares near Falset on the property known as Mas d'en Billo, which is why he named his first wine Billo. In 2009 he decided to make another wine with grapes from another 80 year-old sloped vineyard, Des Nivell, which he sold nearly in its entirety to the US.

Blai's vineyards get the "garbinada" wind which works a quite well to keep the vines fresh, especially during the hot summers that Priorat sees. Eventually, he would like to build a cellar out on the property. But, he's currently quite happy working full time at Cecilio and selling half of his grapes to it while his 8,000 bottles a year on the side continue.

Blai Ferré Just
owner

Blai Ferré Just
Gratallops

Visits: Not currently open for public visits
Contact: blaiferrejust@yahoo.es

Billo 2010 is light in the nose with touches of red fruits and dark cherries. The body opens up with a bit more tannic, drier structure and is sweeter overall. Acids still come up a little and carry in to the finish a bit as well as a touch of smokiness.
25% Grenache, 35% Syrah, 20% Carignan, 10% Cab Sauvignon

 | 14% | 9-10€

Des Nivell 2010 plays off the Billo and adds an oaked structure to it, bringing up more minerality in the nose. The body is well-structured and holds its equilibrium, expanding on the dark cherry flavors. The finish is larger and lingers more, but would pair well with larger dishes. As it decants, more licorice and mint aspects comes in to play.
80% Grenache/Hairy Grenache, 20% Carignan

 | 14,5% | 22-24€

Xavi Buil
owner

GPS
41.2052
0.774267

Buil & Giné
Gratallops, *Carretera Gratallops-La Vilella Baixa, km 2*

Visits: Drop-in tastings are possible at the shop from Monday to Saturday from 10 am to 7pm, and Sunday from 10am to 3pm, but it's always better to book ahead. The cost is 10€ for visit and tasting of three wines and 35€ for a more detailed visit with owner Xavier Buil which includes a tasting of all of their wines in the VIP room with tapas.
Contact: 977839810 | info@builgine.com
Website: www.builgine.com
Languages: English, French, German

Leaving Gratallops and heading towards La Vilella Baixa there are several new, modern wineries that stand out along the road, but none is larger than Buil & Giné. It stands on a bend of the road, topping the mountain with four levels of winery production all wrapped in the local slate stones.

The founder of the winery is Falset native, Xavier Buil i Giné, whose grandfather used to be the president of the co-operative in Falset. In 1996 Xavier decided to start making his own wines in the DOQ Priorat. Initially renting space at the Gratallops collective, in 2005 he built his own winery with the help of an investor. Located at the heart of Priorat and designed to produce wines in a completely gravity fed manner, it was conceived from the start to receive visitors.

They produce about 150,000 bottles a year in all the appellations they work in (DOQ Priorat, DO Montsant, DO Rueda, and DO Toro), and about 80% of the grapes they use come from 33ha of vineyards they own. All their wines are available to buy in their large tasting room where they welcome visitors and sell products such as the gourmet Priorat Natur line that includes vermouth, olive oil, marmalades, nuts, and other tasty products. Additionally, they have a large banquet room on the top floor for events, as well as an exhibition hall and courses on wine tasting.

Joan Giné Rosat 2008 has a nose of cherry and light cola aromas. The body is surprisingly smooth and even tempered, not the least bit sweet, but lingers in to the finish a bit.
Grenache, Merlot
 | 13,5% | 9.25€

Joan Giné Blanc 2011 has a nose of white fruits and is generally summery. The body has slightly bitter elements with a somewhat buttery texture overall and a touch of lemon peel that pulls out in to a fresh, clean finish.
White Grenache, Macabeu, Pedro Ximénez
 | 14% | 12.35€

Giné Giné 2011 has a nose that speaks of dark cherries and very ripe fruits. The body is bright, relatively fresh and carries a large degree of acidity. While not a large or deep wine, it still shows the Priorat character and would work well for general food pairings.
Grenache, Carignan
🔴 | 14,5% | 10.50€

Joan Giné 2007 is aged in small French oak barrels. The nose comes up somewhat fresh, but at the same time carries some jammy fruit flavors. The body is a bit large with tannins and the minerality picks up in the finish that's quite dry overall.
Grenache, Cab Sauvignon
🔴 | 14% | 18€

Pleret 2003 is aged in new French oak. The nose is large, full of slight vanilla elements, but also dark fruits and a hint of herbs at the bottom of it that really lights up the senses. Well balanced on the palate, it has a pinch of spiciness as it approaches the finish as well as some small tobacco elements and smooth chocolate. As it breathes, the mineral aspects com up stronger. The tannins linger in to the finish a bit which sticks around a little.
Grenache, Carignan, Cab Sauvignon, Syrah, Merlot
🔴 | 14% | 34.75€

Pleret Blanc Dolç has a lovely nose of violets and other floral elements as well as a touch of mandarin. The body is quite light and floats on the palate with aspects of orange blossoms and dried apricots. The finish picks up citrus elements as it clears out.
Macabeu, White Grenache, Pedro Ximénez
🟠 | 15% | 23.70€

BUIL & GINÉ

Rafel Gauchola studied enology at the institute in Falset back in the 1990s. He worked for some time at various large cellars in the region before deciding to embark on his own wine venture and planting vineyards in Gratallops in 1997. With planting more vines in 2004, this eventually yielded his first vintage in 2007. He only uses grapes from his own 2.3 hectares of vineyards divided in two plots, La Solana del Melitón and Les Manyetes, and makes one wine in a small cellar in the village of La Vilella Baixa. In being faithful to the land, they've had the "vi de vila" certification since 2009.

The winery and the wine they make is named after a warm wind that blows from the south on summer days, and which reaches their vineyards. Now while they've had several vintages, the production of their one wine remains very small at just 3000 a year.

Rafel Gauchola
owner & enolog

GPS
41.221826
0.761219

Bujorn
La Vilella Baixa, *Carrer Sant Pere de Dalt, 19*

Visits: Not currently open for public visits
Contact: 619437576, 656355663 | bujorn@tinet.cat
Website: www.bujorn.cat

Bujorn 2009 is fermented in open-top oak barrels and then aged for 12 months in the same barrels. The nose shows black pepper as well as touches of sage and other herbs. While initially spicy in the body, it presents violet elements from the Carignan as it breathes. The finish lingers and is dry with a pronounced minerality.

66% Carignan, 17% Grenache, 17% Cab Sauvignon

 | 14,5% | 14-16€ |

Joan Sangenís
owner & enolog

GPS
41.188178
0.855576

Cal Pla

Porrera, *Carrer Prat de la Riba, 1*

Visits: Call to reserve in advance. Visits include a tour of the cellar and a tasting of three wines for 6€ per person with 2-20 people per visit.
Contact: 977828125, 606187431 | joan.sangenis@terra.es
Website: www.cellercalpla.com

Joan Sangenís' family has been making bulk wine at home for at least eight generations in the cellar of Cal Pla, a house that's mentioned in documents dating back to 1814. But it wasn't until 1996 that Joan, upon finishing his enology studies, decided to expand the family cellar with a modern winery facility down the street and started bottling the wines. Joan has changed things up a bit to take advantage of all the modern conveniences while still producing wine that his early 19th century ancestors would be quite proud to drink.

Despite all the hardships that village life has set upon the inhabitants of Porrera, Joan's family has managed to continue production throughout the centuries, being set back by phylloxera, but then starting over again with planting new vines. Historically, they had only made bulk wines up in their lovely old cellar with its arched ceilings. But, in 1996, they switched to producing bottled wines and eventually joining the DOQ appellation for Priorat.

They currently produce about 80,000 bottles a year the majority of which are red wines, but they also make a white and even a rosé.

Old family home

Mas d'en Compte Blanc 2008 shows a nose that's initially strong in oak, but lets a bit of minerality develop as it decants. The body is smooth on the palate with a touch of saltiness and minerality. Overall braced well with acidity that carries in to the finish.

50% White Grenache, 25% Xarel•lo, 25% Piquepoul

🟡 | 13,5% | 12€

Cal Pla Negre 2008 sees 12 months in the barrel. It has a good degree of dark fruits on the nose, but is still generally light in character and fresh. The body brings up a very enjoyable mix of acidity and fruit from the nose as well as a touch of smokiness and stoniness. The finish comes up a touch acidic, but well balanced overall. A good wine for meals or on its own.

Grenache, Carignan, Cab Sauvignon

🔴 | 14,5% | 12€

Mas d'en Compte Negre 2008 is a blend from their old vines. The nose has dark fruits, but with a strong aromatic minerality. The body expands upon the minerality and backs it up with a brace of tannins. While stronger in the mouth than the Negre, it's still light and balanced and lingers pleasantly in the mouth past the finish. The Carignan comes from a 60 year-old vineyard at 450m.

50% Grenache, 40% Carignan, 10% Cab Sauvignon

🔴 | 14,5% | 18€ | ✨

Planots 2008 is from a 100 year-old vineyard planted by Joan's grandfather right after phylloxera. The nose is complex with red fruits and a mineral slate aspect that's a bit different from others due to it being from a soil with more quartz. The body basically bathes in the minerality lovingly and embraces its locale, carrying out in to the finish.

50% Grenache, 50% Carignan

🔴 | 14% | 50€

Francesc Capafons
owner

GPS
41.154283
0.802613

Capafons-Ossó

Falset, *Camí vell de Gratallops, Masia Esplanes*

Visits: Available by appointment at a cost of 25€ per person and include a lengthy, in-depth tour of the vineyards, and tasting of their wines. Budget a solid half a day as the experience is quite immersive and personal. English tours are available via tour guide Rachel Ritchie.
Leave the Car: For those who wish to arrive by train, the winery owners can pick you up from the Falset-Marça station with prior notice.
Contact: 977831201,656352029(English) | cellers@capafons-osso.com
Website: www.capafons-osso.com
Languages: English

From the moment you first meet Francesc Capafons and hear him talk about Priorat, you notice that something is different. He and his wife, Montserrat Ossó are locals to Falset and you can immediately see it in the way Francesc intimately knows the land while taking the visitor on a tour. He can not only point out every stone and herb, but even the different subtypes. It's not a surprise, though, as Francesc and Montserrat's marriage brought together five generations of winemaking history in the area and naturally, their son, Francesc Xavier has picked up the reigns to head up the enology work in the cellar these days. After years of growing grapes and selling them to a local collective, they made their first vintage in 1991 and now make nearly a dozen wines in both the DOQ Priorat and DO Montsant as their vineyards are in between the two, including 22 in Priorat.

When driving over one part of their 60 hectare property it becomes readily apparent that in addition to planting new vines that respect the forest and the mountains, they've also worked a great deal to recuperate the old ones that were already there. You can see their organic production easily up in the vineyards where all manner of plants and herbs are growing amongst the vines each with a healthy respect for one another.

A visit to Capafons-Ossó is not only a visit to a winery and a tasting of wines, but also a unique chance to experience the place from the immersive perspective of locals.

Enllaç 2008 spends seven months in new oak. This initially comes across a good deal in the nose, but as it breathes, an underlying minerality comes up as well. It's light on the palate with touches of citric elements and a touch of heat that builds in to pleasant acids in the finish.

60% Viognier, 40% White Grenache

🟡 | 14% | 22-25€

Sirsell 2007 has a warm and deep nose of tobacco and a hint of almonds, cherries, and underlying minerality. The body is full of red fruits, surprisingly bright, and a touch sweet from the main red fruit element. The finish is smooth with a most interesting hint of vanilla and herbal elements.

40% Grenache, 29% Merlot, 17% Cab Sauvignon, 7% Carignan, 7% Syrah

 | 15,5% | 14-16€

Masos d'en Cubells 2004 opens with a subtle, slate-filled nose that quietly states its minerality. The minerality is quite active in the body as well as acidity. The fruits in the body hint at very mature, aged components that show a very good growing year.

30% Grenache, 30% Cab Sauvignon, 25% Syrah, 15% Carignan

 | 14,5% | 26-29€

Mas de Masos 2002 has a nose with a solid foundation in slate minerality, but with great wild herbal aspects of chamomile, sage, and rosemary. The body is wonderfully complex, rich and balanced. While immediately approachable and easy to drink, it also has wondrous depth. The tannins kick up, but it shows mature, delicious fruit that are not easy to put in to one character.

30% Hairy Grenache, 25% Grenache, 15% Carignan, 25% Cab Sauvignon, 5% Syrah

 | 14% | 36-40€ | ✹

Mas de Masos Dolç 2007 is the result of a heat wave that made the grapes raisin too quickly and thus a dessert wine was born. The nose is wonderfully buttery and smooth like caramel. Despite the high sugar, the minerality still comes through. Light on the palate, it lacks all the cloying sweet elements typical in dessert wines and is refreshing in the finish. Sadly, only 700 bottles were made of which 200 remain.

60% Hairy Grenache, 40% Cab Sauvignon

 | 15,5% | 35€ | ✹

CAPAFONS-OSSÓ

In 1996 enology professor Toni Alcover, who is now the DOQ Priorat's president, started making the Fra Fulcó wines in La Vilella Alta with agriculture engineer Francesc Sànchez-Bas started and other partners. Over time the society dissolved and Fra Fulcó stopped being produced, but Francesc continued with Cartoixa as a solo venture, making his first vintage in 2000.

Sharing space between several old stone buildings in La Vilella Alta including Francesc's mother's family house, Cartoixa de Montsalvat currently produces 12-20,000 bottles a year, with Roser Amorós as the enolog. All of this production comes from around 10 hectares of vineyards they farm organically, while still buying some grapes from local growers.

Montgarnatx 2004 opens with a dark fruit nose. In the body, it falls in to the sweeter style of dry wine that some in Priorat make. Acidity comes up a little and in to the finish.
70% Grenache, 30% Carignan

🔴 | 14% | 25€

Francesc Sànchez-Bas
owner

GPS
41.225897
0.780056

Cartoixa de Montsalvat
La Vilella Alta, *Carrer Ereta, 10*

Visits: It's free to visit and taste the wines with a purchase. Call ahead to reserve a time.
Contact: 977839299 | correu@cellerscartoixa.com
Website: www.cellerscartoixa.com

Blanc de Montsalvat 2009 has a slightly sweet, mineral nose that's crisp and fresh, with a touch of mint at the bottom of it. In the body, heavy astringency appears initially but with a good degree of acidity. The body is full with a slight bitterness out to the finish. With air, a caramel aspect develops and the texture gets quite thick with petrol notes.
65% Macabeu, 35% White Trepat

🟡 | 14% | 18€ |

Costers de Vilolla 2004 blends grapes only from old vines. It's initially deep with darker fruits to the nose. The body doesn't have as toys with being a bit deeper before the acids come up a bit carrying slightly in to the finish.
90% Carignan, 10% Grenache

🔴 | 14,5% | 34€

Moritz Kroning
enolog

GPS
41.163342
0.76577

Casa Gran del Siurana
Bellmunt del Priorat, *Carrer Major, 3*

Visits: Not currently open for public visits
Contact: 669841857,932233022 | jalentorn@castilloperelada.com
Website: www.casagrandelsiurana.com
Languages: English, German

The rented cellar of Casa Gran is set in the very drab Bellmunt cooperative building, where they use the old cement tanks as barrel-aging rooms. But it's the vineyards that are the most striking aspect of their production. Spread amongst terraces of red clay and slate and along the Siurana River, they're an impressive site to see in the Southern region.

These two properties (La Fredat with the terraces and llicorella soils, and Casa Gran down by the river with clay soils) form the basis of this new winery that was started in 2000 with their first vintage in 2004. The majority of it is now owned by Empordà wine giant, Castillo de Perelada with Jordi Alentorn owning a smaller share as well as running the day to day aspects of the winery. For anyone who has been up north to Empordà and seen Perelada's Garbet vineyard, you will notice a striking similarity to La Fredat which is due to the fact that it formed the blueprint for developing the Garbet terraces.

The namesake Casa Gran property, while not as stunning as the terraces, isn't to be overlooked either. At the heart of it is a very large, early 18th century stone house that was built by the Priorat monks to spend summers there. This fertile area with alluvial clay soils from the river provided them with a crucial breadbasket area where they grew many crops and, while not owned by the monks anymore,

Jordi Alentorn Torné in the vineyards

still provides a great wealth of agricultural production today that includes Casa Gran's vineyards which surround the old house.

From the 18 hectares that these Priorat vineyards cover and from grapes they buy from growers in Bellmunt and El Lloar, they produce 200,000 bottles annually. They make three labels that see a great deal of exposure through international export around the world. Since 2007 their enolog is Moritz Kroning.

GR-174 2011 is named after the trail that crosses the vineyards. The nose has strong red fruit components with hints of violets. The finish is fresh and comes up clean, with darker berry aromas. It's best approached as a friendly young wine for meals, and is also their most popular wine of which they make 100,000 bottles.
40% Cab Sauvignon, 35% Grenache, 25% Carignan

● | 15% | 9€ | ⚖

Cruor 2007 sees 12 months of French oak in a mix of new and old barrels. Despite the year, it's still a bit tight in the glass. The nose has light fig elements and transfers in to the body well with bright, red fruits. The body is rich with tobacco and pleasing acids, as well as a degree of spiciness but still refreshing.
30% Grenache, 30% Cab Sauvignon, 20% Syrah, 10% Carignan, 10% Merlot

● | 14,5% | 18€

Gran Cruor 2007 opens with dark fruits and wafts of vanilla to the nose. Spices also come up which then carry in to the body. Soft on the palate, minerality comes in to a play a good deal. Overall, it's quite smooth and lingers in to the finish a good deal.
90% Syrah, 10% Carignan

● | 15% | 30€

Castellet is one of the Porrera wineries that are lucky enough to lay claim to some of the very old vineyards that dot the steep hills of the valley to the east of the village in the direction of La Garranxa area. Out amongst the llicorella stones, scraggly vines eke out an existence and, for decades have been making intensely flavorful grapes that Castellet is able to use in their wines. In total, they harvest from about four and half hectares of vineyards, of which 25% have 85 year-old Carignan vines.

They started formally bottling their wines in 2005 with a small release of just 1,500 bottles. In the five years prior to this, they were experimenting a great deal with the grape blends. They're still a small production winery with a total of 7,000 bottles a year between their three red wines and about 30% of their grapes being sold to other wineries. Their third wine, Empit Selecció, is a limited edition from their oldest vines with Vi de vila certification.

Their cellar in the center of Porrera is compact and charming with their main stainless steel tanks up top and down through a door in the floor, their barrels.

Jordi Castellet
owner & enolog

GPS
41.188271
0.854972

Castellet
Porrera, *Font de dalt 11*

Visits: They offer tours that include a tour of their cellar, vineyards, tasting, and a bottle of Ferral as a gift to take home for 10€ a person. Call to make a reservation.
Contact: 977828044, 630849874 | cellercastellet@yahoo.es
Website: www.cellercastellet.cat

Ferral 2010 is named after the type of lli-corella soil in the vineyard. It has a nose with dark fruits and light hints of slate. The body brings up a good brace of acids to compliment the minerality that runs throughout it as well as a trace of bitter chocolate, and leather.
50% Grenache/Hairy Grenache, 21% Cab Sauvignon, 19% Syrah, 10% Merlot

● | 15% | 11€

Empit 2011 gives off herbal aspects in the nose. Hints of rosemary are mixed with anise. The body comes together in a different fashion, carrying the herbal elements from the nose. Overall, it has a sweeter character to it. The finish is similar though with a dry texture and pleasant herbal elements that stick around quite pleasantly.
52% Grenache, 25% Cab Sauvignon, 23% Carignan

● | 15% | 15€

August Vicent
owner & enolog

GPS
41.193071
0.775662

Cecilio
Gratallops, *Carrer Piró, 28*

Visits: They're open every day all day (except Sundays and holidays in the afternoon) for drop in visits and tastings which are free of charge. They also offer full tours of their vineyards and old cellar by appointment. Groups are welcome to a maximum of 20 people.
Contact: 977839507,977839181 | celler@cellercecilio.com
Website: www.cellercecilio.com

August Vicent puts it most succinctly when he says, "We may not be the best, but we were the first." Active since 1942, Cecilio was indeed the first registered cellar in the DOQ Priorat. Of course back in those days, bulk wine sales made up the majority of their output until 1997 when they started focusing mostly on bottle sales. And, although it's hard to tell who makes the best wines of Priorat, Cecilio does make some with the best price to quality ratio.

Now, from about nine hectares, they produce around 30,000 bottles a year, primarily for direct sale at the winery, although like most wineries in the area, 2012 saw their production cut by 30% due to the very dry growing season. Their vineyards are in primarily in Gratallops as well as one in el Lloar.

Located right on the main street of Gratallops and easy to find, Cecilio has the distinction of being one of the best appointed wineries for people to visit. They have constant opening hours throughout the week,tastings free of charge, as well as a small museum in the back of the winery that pays tribute to their many generations of making wine in Priorat. If you encounter the extremely friendly August on the right day, you might even get the chance to try some of the very old vi ranci that they've been aging for decades.

Wolves of Cecilio and Gratallops

Blanc 2011 is both light in the nose and body. Very easy to drink and quite fresh overall, the minerality comes up in the finish, but it stays overall quite fresh.

100% White Grenache

🟡 | 13,5% | 9€ | ⚖️

Negre 2010 has a rather light nose that betrays just a touch of the acidity that comes up more in the body. Quite easy to drink and very even tempered young wine that would pair well with a great many dishes.

100% Grenache, 20% Cab Sauvignon, 20% Carignan, 10% Syrah

🔴 | 14% | 7€ | ⚖️

L'Espill 2007 receives one year of aging in French oak. The nose has deeper dark fruits. The body is decently large, but again with an easygoing character. The finish is light and carries well. Like their young wine, it presents a very approachable bottle but with character and would be versatile for many meals.

60% Grenache, 30% Cab Sauvignon, 10% Carignan

🔴 | 14% | 15€ | ⚖️

Their wine museum

GPS
41.193038
0.774948

Cesca Vicent
Gratallops, *Carretera. Gratallops-La Vilella Baixa*

Visits: Guests can visit the winery and taste the wines Monday through Friday. Visits are free of charge.
Contact: 610536573,637516314 | info@cescavicentpriorat.com
Website: cescavicentpriorat.com

It's an unassuming building on the northeast corner of Gratallops where Francesca "Cesca" Vicent Robert set up her winery back in 2000. But, despite the compact form both inside and out, this is where they make all their wines with Emili Esteve as their enolog. They only use grapes from their 13 hectares of vineyards, some of which have been cultivated with vines as far back as the 15th century. And, if the name "Vicent" seems familiar, it's because she is the sister of August and daughter of Cecilio Vicent who started the Cecilio cellar just around the corner.

Since 1999, they've practiced strict controls on how they cultivate their vineyards, taking care to work in an organic fashion respectful with the environment and harvesting everything by hand. When they started the winery they commissioned a soil analysis of their property and they discovered to learn more about the conditions in which their grapes grow. They discovered that their vineyards are on 11 different soils, a diversity that has allowed them to plant the types of grapes that can best express each of them.

Keeping this goal of showcasing the locale, they harvest, ferment and age each grape and vineyard separately. For the wines that are aged, they use about half French and half American oak barrels.

Cabaler 2009 is fermented as well as aged in the barrels for 3-4 months which creates a large nose, but one that doesn't overpower. It has citric notes in the nose and plays well across the palate. Smooth and enjoyable, it presents apricot flavors and white fruits that eventually pull in to a tight, satisfying finish.
White Grenache, Macabeu, Trepat Blanc, Trobat
🟡 | 13% | 7€

Cesca Vicent 2010 shows dark berries in the nose as well as a hint of vanilla and smokiness. More than half of the wine spends six months in the barrels which give it a large body that slides over the palate, but the finish comes up quite dry overall. While somewhat young, it's surprisingly well balanced.
Grenache, Cab Sauvignon, Syrah, and Merlot
 | 15% | 7€

Lo Piot 2007 has a nose with a hint of pine and structured elements. There are very delicate aromas and it receives 12 months in oak. The body is strong and fleshy in the mouth, but balanced with a decently high degree of acidity that sticks through in to the finish. It is very food friendly overall but better suited for larger meals, especially from the grill.
Cab Sauvignon, Grenache
 | 15,5% | 11€

Abat Domènech 2007 has a nose with a touch of mineral elements and a small degree of acidity. The wine sees 12 months in the barrels. Bright in the body, it is rather hot and spicy overall, but is still tasty and agreeable. Dry in to the finish, the acidity picks up to pair with many dishes, but especially those with a larger flavor such as roasted pork and lamb or even a roasted chicken with herbs.
50% Cab Sauv, 50% Grenache/Carignan/Syrah/Merlot
 | 15% | 16€

Vell Segle XX is a special dessert wine with a composition of mainly Grenache and a tiny bit of Syrah. It is aged for 10 years in a very unique combination of barrels made from chestnut, oak, acacia, and cherry. They only make 300 bottles that are 500ml in volume, with a label designed by famous Catalan painter Jordi Rollan.
Grenache, Syrah
 | 16% | 23.50€

Dic Duran
enolog

GPS
41.18685
0.855195

Cims de Porrera

Porrera, *Carretera de Torroja*

Visits: Available everyday with a maximum of 20 people, there is no cost to visit the winery, but they conduct visits on a *very* limited basis. Call to see what's available and make a reservation.
Contact: 977828233 | info@cimsdeporrera.com
Website: cimsdeporrera.com
Languages: English, French

In 1994 Porrera suffered heavy floods that destroyed most of the crops. Famous Catalan singer Lluís Llach--whose mother was from Porrera--decided to do something to reactivate the local economy. So in 1996 he started a winery at the local cooperative. He also got Josep Lluís Pérez on board, one of the pioneers of Priorat's rebirth who had founded Mas Martinet a decade earlier.

The cooperative, which had been built in 1932 and enlarged in 1954, was in decline in the 1990s with their members barely making a living selling their grapes off to larger wineries. So, the new Cims de Porrera winery decided to buy grapes from them at above market prices and make use of the old building to make high quality wines. Sometime later though, Lluís Llach and Enric Costa established their own winery in town (Vall Llach) and sold their share of Cims de Porrera to the Suqué family of Empordà wine giant, Castillo de Perelada.

These days, it's Josep Lluís's son Adrià Pérez who manages the winery and takes care of the enology. With his cousin Marc he also produces a separate line of wines under the label Les Cousins. The two of them work alongside Dic Duran, who exudes an exacting and hypnotic precision in the cellar like you'd see with a classical concert conductor.

While the main portion of the coop building is basic in its layout with large tanks, the lower portion where they perform barrel aging is quite fascinating. This subterranean area used to be the old concrete tanks where the cooperative would age the wines in bulk. Now that Cims de Porrera ages all of their vineyards separately prior to the final blend, they use these tanks to store the barrels. Some time ago, Dic took a hammer and saw to the walls to craft a labyrinth of wine and barrels.

Until 2004 the "Clàssic" Cims de Porrera wine was a blend of 70% Grenache and 30% Carignan but in 2005 they decided to "divorce" the two varietals and bottle them separately. In addition to that they now make different single vineyard wines each year that have a very limited production. Currently Cims de Porrera culls their selection from 30 hectares of vineyards that are all located in the municipality and produce about 15,000 bottles a year.

Solanes 2007 has a nose that pulls out elderberry aromas with a touch of black currant at the bottom. The body is initially tart with black pepper developing as it breathes. While a touch jammy to the finish, it's overall fresh and invigorating.

45% Carignan, 30% Grenache, 15% Cab Sauvignon, 10% Merlot/Syrah

● | 14,5% | 15€

"Clàssic" Garnatxa 2006 is sourced from their 100 year-old vines. It has a dark, spicy nose with touches of pepper to it along with hints of sage. The body is rich with tobacco and a balanced acidity. As it breathes, an aspect of bitter lime comes in to the nose and it lightens up a good deal on the palate to pull in to a dry finish. While full in the body, it's a wonderfully classy wine.

100% Grenache

● | 14,5% | 43€ |

"Clàssic" Caranyana 2007 has a dark and lustrous nose that is infinitely silky. There are mineral and herbal elements present, but they're quite downplayed. The body is spicy but plush and fills in the mouth with dark fruits. The minerality initially gets tossed aside for rich tannins and acids which float on in to the finish leaving a puff of dark, ripe blackberry on the palate as they go. Light tobacco and coffee elements grow and are carried by a constantly shifting buttery aspect. A highly complex and beautiful wine.

100% Carignan

● | 14,5% | 45-50€ |

One of the newest wineries to join the DOQ Priorat, Clos 93 has quite scenic vineyards in El Lloar set up against the red, rocky bluffs of the Montsant range. This area is called Rogerals and takes its name from the red color of the rocks. From there you can see caves that soldiers hid in during the Spanish Civil War. Amongst scrubby bushes and old olive trees, their vineyards are a large departure from the tightly manicured and heavily sculpted vineyards of their neighbor Torres Priorat. The five hectares of their vineyards grow on both red clay soil as well as llicorella.

The winery started as a project of young enolog Rubén Sabaté, who works at Clos Figueras, to make a casual and approachable wine that he could have when going out with his friends instead of beer. This wine became l'Interrogant, meaning, "question mark" in Catalan and they produced their first vintage in 2011. They produce 3200 bottles currently, and they have plans to release a second label which will be an aged wine called, L'Admiració, "exclamation mark" in Catalan. They are also making high quality oil from the trees in their property, made with local olive varieties Farga, Rojals and Arbequina.

Pepo García
owner

GPS
41.185564
0.750428

Clos 93
El Lloar, *Carrer Nou, 26*

Visits: Call ahead for reservations and pricing. They also offer tasting classes with a minimum of six people.
Contact: 665287433, 620215770 | clos93@clos93.com
Website: www.clos93.com

L'Interrogant (?) 2011 has a touch of butter to the nose and is neither heavy nor hot with a slight licorice aspect developing with some time open. While the body starts with a good deal of minerality, the soils have changed the nature of the wine quite a bit to soften the tannins and make for a food friendly wine.
Grenache, Carignan, Cab Sauvignon

● | 15% | 11€12€ |

Rubén's brother Josep Maria and their uncle Pepo García who owns the vineyards complete the Clos 93 team. The cellar down in the village of El Lloar is quite compact. It was built in the basement of Pepo García's parents' home which used to house a bakery. There, they have a very nice tasting area set in to the space where the oven had been carved in to the bedrock below the village.

Not only is Clos Berenguer the most southern winery in the DOQ Priorat, but it has one of the most unique settings being that the cellar is built in to one of the old mines that are dotted around this southern area. While the magnesium that they were digging up ran out, it left a fantastic place to age barrels and store wines.

Started in 1999 with construction of the cellar completed in 2000, they now lay claim to 19 hectares of vineyards and produce enough grapes to have plenty to sell off to other wineries. It's a lovely setting that should come as no surprise, as it was designed by the architect owner, Francesc Berengué. Situated down a winding trail that takes you through the short pines and other trees in the area, it would make a great spot for visitors if they weren't completely unaware of the enotourism potential this winery has.

Francesc Berengué
owner

GPS
41.145489
0.715869

Clos Berenguer
El Molar, *Carretera El Masroig-El Molar, km 4.6*

Visits: Visits are free and there is always someone onsite, but to taste the wines, visitors need to buy the bottles.
Contact: 606453536, 977361390 │ info@closberenguer.com
Website: www.closberenguer.com

Rosat 2011 has a nose that brings up elements of cedar and cola. The body has a lot of muddled spices to it, picking up cinnamon and other elements with a generally fresh finish, although it will put off most people.
Merlot
● | 13,5% | 7€

Blanc de Botes 2007 has an aspect to the nose that flirts with being mineral in overall quality, but is a bit different and more acrid. The body is light overall and generally well balanced, but the sharp elements from the nose come in to play and set up a different kind of acidity that is hard to get past.
50% White Grenache, 40% Xarel•lo, 10% P. Ximénez
● | 13,5% | 7€

Dominic Bairaguet
Paco Castillo
owners

GPS
41.188154
0.855246

Clos Dominic

Porrera, *Carrer Pau Casals, 4*

Visits: Available on weekends, call ahead for a reservation. The cost is 8€ per person with a maximum of 20 people.
Contact: 977828215, 608843376 | clos_dominic@hotmail.com
Website: debrujasyvino.blogspot.com

As is the story with many of the wineries in Porrera, Clos Dominic is a relatively small endeavor that was created by two people who fell in love with the landscape of Priorat and after spending many summers in Porrera ended up settling down. Dominic Bairaguet and her husband Paco Castillo say they started making wine in 2002 "like the Flintstones", as they only had a couple of tanks and six barrels in the basement of their home that used to be a baker's oven. Their current production cellar is in a building that's been a cellar for the last 150 years in the village.

Dominic and Paco, along with their daughter Ingrid taking care of the enology duties, now produce about 13-15,000 bottles a year out of their seven hectares of vineyards. They make all the wines with natural fermentation. While not explosive in growth, they've come a long way from the six barrels that they started out with a decade ago and the wines continually receive very high scores from wine critics both local and international.

They also do an excellent job of showing visitors where the final wine in the bottle comes from. Visits always start out with a trip to and a walk through their very old vineyards in the valley to the east of Porrera. Once seeing these old vines clinging to the slopes and the very unadulterated area where several wineries grow their vines alongside the river, visitors then head back to the cellar to have a guided tasting through several of their wines. All told, it takes up the better part of a morning for those looking to experience an immersive cellar tour in Priorat.

Clos Petó 2010 has chocolate and dark fruit nose. The body is large in tannins with strong plum aspects which all carry quite well in to the finish. Despite the overall strength of it, it's a very approachable wine.

50% Carignan, 40% Cab Sauv, 5% Merlot, 5% Grenache

 | 15% | 15€ |

Vinyes Baixes 2006 has a more elegant nose with dusty minerality and slight hazelnut textures. The body is buoyant with more acidity. With air, the hazelnut comes up more and more a touch of a bitter backbone to it. While larger, it would still pair well with meals.

50% Merlot, 20% Cab Sauv, 20% Grenache, "Others"

 | 14.5% | 25-30€

Vinyes Altes 2006 has a buttery, smooth, almond laced nose. The body is again large and expresses the soil well. Delicate, dried fruits such as figs and prunes permeate throughout it and the finish lingers nicely.

Grenache, Carignan

● | 14.5% | 30-40€

Barrel cellar

Daphne Glorian
owner & enolog

GPS
41.192782
0.775989

Clos Erasmus
Gratallops, *Carrer de la Font, 1*

Visits: Not currently open for public visits
Contact: 977839022,977839426 | info@closerasmus.com
Website: www.closerasmus.com

French-Swiss wine merchant Daphne Glorian didn't start out with the intention of having one of the most renowned cellars in Priorat. She met René Barbier and Álvaro Palacios at a wine fair and they convinced her to join them in going to Priorat to make world-class wines. She sold everything, arrived in Priorat, and purchased a small vineyard in Gratallops. As the story goes, all of the people in this initial group seeking to revitalize Priorat produced their first vintage in the same warehouse in 1989. Five of them went on to create their own wineries, and that old warehouse became Clos Mogador. The international acclaim these first wines received surpassed the group's expectations--for instance Clos Erasmus received 99 Parker points in 1994 turning it into a cult wine (since then it has received the much-coveted 100 points on several occasions).

This original purchase of old vine Grenache in Gratallops led to the founding of the winery, as Daphne says the quality of the grapes is what made her wines great. From the start all of the vineyards were farmed organically and eventually in 2004, they took it one step further to become biodynamic as well. But, despite earning the absolute highest of marks from wine critics, Daphne has kept her winery quite small producing only about 3,000 bottles of her Clos Erasmus and about 10,000 of Laurel. Also, in a quest to make a fresher style of wine, in 2012 she has started experimenting with 700 liter amphorae for aging.

Today, Daphne splits her time between Gratallops and New York as she's married to star US importer Eric Solomon. Since 2004 the winery has been managed by one of the most talented enologs in Priorat, Esther Nin--who also produces her own line of wines with her partner. The vineyards total 10.5 compact hectares with a strong emphasis on Grenache, with small amounts of Syrah. All of the wines are produced in Gratallops at an unassuming cellar in the village which is only marked by the silhouette of 15th century Dutch scholar Erasmus of Rotterdam from which the flagship wine takes its name.

Laurel 2010 has a mineral nose with hints of earthy root vegetables. It embraces the palate with shimmering dark fruits. The body takes on flavors of raspberry with a texture of chocolate mousse that leads in to a dry finish. With a decent amount of decanting, it also develops a burnt caramel aspect.

70% Grenache, 20% Syrah, 10% Cab Sauvignon

● | 15% | 30€

Clos Erasmus 2010 is made from the three properties of les Escales, Sucarrats, and Aubagues. It has a gentle, soft nose that pulls together all the common elements of wines in the region in an understated manner with electric, lively fruits at the bottom of it. The body is warm, taking over the palate in soft, direct manners while at the same time being plush and balanced with acids and tannins. It picks up a floral, violet element as it slides in the finish, which then drifts off as the finish lingers with soft acidity. As it decants, the minerality picks up a great deal. In an elegant manner, it shows off the soil very well without overwhelming the palate.

70% Grenache, 30% Syrah

● | 15% | 140€ | ✸

Clay amphora and oak tanks

Christopher Cannan
Anne Cannan
owners

GPS
41.192205
0.777548

Clos Figueras
Gratallops, *Carrer de la Font, 38*

Visits: They offer visits with a tasting of two of their wines for 12€ a person and a longer visit with a tasting of their four wines for 75€ for a whole group of up to 12 people. Prior reservation via phone or their website is necessary. They also have a shop selling theirs and other wines and the restaurant Les Figueres open on weekends and holidays, serving local specialties with high quality ingredients.
Contact: 977262373,627471732 | info@closfigueras.com
Website: www.closfigueras.com,www.lesfigueres.com
Languages: English, French, German, Italian

Having founded top quality wine export company, Europvin in 1978, Christopher Cannan first encountered the wines of Priorat in 1983 thanks to a bottle by Scala Dei that had made its way to San Francisco. Shortly after, he started exporting those wines to various countries. Some years later he met Álvaro Palacios who told him about his project to revitalize winemaking in Priorat, and through him Réné Barbier came into the picture as well. Skeptical at first, Christopher was quickly convinced after tasting a bottle of Clos Mogador and saw the immense potential for the region to create world-class wines.

In 1997 he and his wife, Charlotte purchased the Clos Figueras estate of 10 hectares in Gratallops with the help of René Barbier. It had been abandoned for some years, so they had to plant some new vines in addition to the older ones they worked to recuperate. In 1999 they already produced their first vintage, only 1,200 bottles, and their wines very quickly garnered some of the highest scores of international wine critics. Also, in 2000 they purchased the adjacent property bringing their estate to 18ha out of which 12 are planted with vines.

Just as you enter the village of Gratallops, coming from the direction of Falset, there is a right turn in to the understated premises of Clos Figueras. Housed in what used to be a large chicken coop, their cellar is, by many standards quite small, but is quite adequate for their current production needs of about 30,000 bottles a year. Below their production cellar sits their barrel aging room. It was originally a water cistern, but once they pumped out the funky water and decades, if not centuries of mud, they found it to be a quite wonderful space to age their wines.

Back up top, in the front half of their production cellar, they're running a charming restaurant on weekends and holidays aptly named, Les Figueres. It has comfortable, outdoor seating with views over the terraced hills and they serve local dishes source from small farmers in the area. Here visitors can grab a tasty bite as well as buy the Clos Figueras wines directly from their shop and also their high-end estate olive oil that's packaged like a classy, aged bottle of Scotch. Currently they produce a white wine, three reds and a sweet entirely made with old-vine Grenache.

Font de la Figuera Blanc 2010 shows floral aromas blended with the smallest hit of summer fruits. It's bright, nearly to a point of bitter in the mouth. It could spend a bit more time in the bottle but is an interesting and unique blend of mainly Viognier that they planted as a result of a mistake by the nursery where they purchased vines that were supposed to be Cabernet Sauvignon.
85% Viognier, 15% White Grenache/Chenin Blanc
| 13,5% | 21€

Font de la Figuera Negre 2008 has a nose that opens up a bit hot and gives off hints of roasted corn. While fruit forward and pronounced on the palate, the finish shows interesting leather notes while closing out.
Grenache, Carignan, Syrah, Cab Sauvignon
| 14,5% | 21€ |

Clos Figueres 2007 takes their 60 year-old Grenache and Carignan grapes and blends them with younger estate vines. It presents delicate boysenberry and blackberry to the nose. The body boasts great minerality, with a texture that drifts back and forth from silky to spicy. It's a strong, complex wine with a definitive backbone that sits lightly on the palate and with a great balance overall.
Grenache, Carignan, Syrah, Mourvèdre, Cab Sauvignon
| 14,5% | 48€

René Barbier IV
owner & enolog

GPS
41.190362
0.771982

Clos Mogador
Gratallops, *Camí Manyetes*

Visits: With a prior reservation, it's possible to visit the winery, vineyards and taste the wines at 25-28€ per person with a maximum of 10 people.
Contact: 977839171 | closmogador@closmogador.com
Website: www.closmogador.com
Languages: English, French, German

Clos Mogador and its founder, René Barbier III, along with his family are undeniably responsible for the reputation and fame that Priorat is privy to today. This original member of the "Big Five" wineries arrived in Priorat in 1979 to begin revitalizing an ancient wine region which has taken decades to attain its current state. But, it was something of a roundabout journey from France to arrive at this point.

The Barbier family history in wine starts back in the 19th century with Léon Barbier I producing bottled wines up in the Vaucluse region of southern France. A massive estate of some 1,500 hectares, they were hit hard by the phylloxera plague in 1880 and moved their enterprise to Catalonia to avoid complete financial ruin.

They founded a new winery in Tarragona, under the name of Léon I's son, René I. The winery was successful for some time and in the 1940's, descendants, Léon II and René II started bottling some of the first wines from Priorat made in more modern production methods, in addition to wines from other regions of Catalonia. The enterprise grew, but René II died prematurely at 50 and the company was bought by a group of "doubtful reputation" during the dictatorship era of Francisco Franco. With the return

Barrel cellar

to democracy, the Barbier family was not in a position at that point to buy back the company and it ended up being bought by others and became the Freixenet winery you see today.

Leaving this past behind them, René III and his wife, Isabelle Meyer sought out a new path in Priorat. Starting in an old warehouse outside of Gratallops for a cellar, with several friends they began replanting terraces and recuperating old ones to eventually have their first release in 1989 as Clos Mogador. This name comes from a novel written by an aunt named, Élisabeth Barbier called, "Les Gens de Mogador" ("The people of Mogador") which chronicles the rise and fall of a family from near Avignon in France on an imaginary estate called, Mogador. They obviously saw it as a fitting name for their renewed family wine enterprise.

Today, they're still making wine in the same warehouse where it all started over 30 years ago and the young vines that were planted back then are now old. Their stunning Clos Mogador property graces countless articles and brochures about Priorat as it illustrates the modern terraces better than no other, and from their 50ha of vineyards they make around 46,000 bottles a year.

Gratallops and vines in autumn

René III has retired from active winemaking though he continues to be involved mainly in the viticulture side of things. René IV (whom people locally call, René Jr.) has been working at the winery alongside his dad since 1992 and has now taken over running it. He says he wants to stay true to the his father's winemaking style and spirit, but he's been introducing some important changes such as not adding any yeast (only native yeast), using fewer new barrels, introducing a selection table, and decreasing the production of Cabernet Sauvignon.

But this wine saga story has no ending as René IV married Sara Pérez, the daughter of Josep Lluís Pérez, founder of the other "Big Five" winery, Mas Martinet that she now manages. Between René IV and Sara, they have not only a handful of wineries but also four children together. When asked if this new generation will continue in their parents' footsteps, the answer is, "We hope so because there is a winery waiting for each of them."

A view of the valley

Nelin 2011 has a light, fleeting nose with soft aromas of taffy and caramel. The body is soft and slightly mineraly, but at the same time a meaty character that lends a great deal of depth to the wine. The finish comes up slightly bitter and marked, but cleanses the palate quite well.
54% White Grenache, 46% Macabeu/Viognier/Pinot Noir/Escanyavella/Pedro Ximenez

 | 14% | 30€

Manyetes 2009 has a buttery minerality to the nose. Excellent fruits come up in the body, bright with minerality, acidity and showing the property very well. A dry, dusty finish, it leaves the palate with excellent remnants of the wine.
90% Carignan, 10% Grenache

 | 14,5% | 50-55€

Clos Mogador 2008 is the first and so far the only certified "Vi de Finca" in Spain, a similar certification to that of Grand Cru in France. It has dark, sultry fruits with a touch of prune to it in the nose. Light on the palate and elegant as hell, it dances across the fruits elements. The body is meaty, nearly chewy, but stops just short before bringing up the lingering acids in the finish with floral, violet hints coming in to play as it decants.
44% Grenache, 25% Carignan, 16% Syrah, 15% Cab Sauv

 | 14,5% | 55-60€

Carles Pastrana,
Mariona Jarqué
owners

GPS
41.190451
0.772422

Clos de l'Obac
Gratallops, *Camí Manyetes*

Visits: They offer tailor-made visits depending for groups of maximum 30 people at a cost of 25€ per person that includes a tasting of their wines. Call ahead for reservations.
Contact: 977839276 | info@costersdelsiurana.com
Website: www.costersdelsiurana.com
Languages: English, French

Given that Carles Pastrana was childhood friends with René Barbier, it should come as little surprise that he and his wife, Mariona Jarqué joined up with René in 1979 to start Clos de l'Obac, one of the original "Big Five" wineries of Priorat. At the time, Carles was a journalist in Tarragona and Mariona was a designer. Carles' family had held on to a small vineyard in Tarragona for generations which helped to plant the seeds for the family to start up their full-fledged winery venture.

Working in the same old warehouse space as Clos Mogador, they released their first wine, Clos de l'Obac in 1989, followed by Miserere in 1990, and Dolç de l'Obac in 1991. These wines were the result of a great deal of recuperation work carried out on a couple of old properties in the area including el Mas d'en Bruno, a 100 hectare estate with a 13th century 5,000 square meter masia that they slowly restored. As Mariona emphasizes, starting the winery from zero was a lot of hard work that in the end paid off.

Today, they occupy the other half of the old warehouse that they started in with Clos Mogador and the others. They've built an impressive cellar over the years that's a tightly integrated, gravity fed production system running over several floors. They produce some 58,000 bottles a year from their 50ha of vineyards, although this can vary a great deal from year to year. All their barrels are decorated by a ceramic cover handcrafted by Gratallops potter, Lluís Riera.

It's easy to see when touring the winery that they take a great deal of care and pride in their wines. They keep the exact same blend each year to better showcase each vintage, and they're also one of the few wineries who change their prices a great deal per vintage, allowing the wine made that year to dictate the market amount. With the wine leftover from each year's blending they make their second line of wines called, Usatge.

Kyrie 2007 has a nose with strong minerality to it that's boosted by the oak aging which emits a slightly sweet shortbread element as it breathes. The body is light and fleeting with the acids coming up quite quickly and freely. A citric element comes in to place at the end which carries in to the finish.
White Grenache, Macabeu, Xarel•lo, Muscat

 | 14% | 50€

Miserere 2004 has a curious, signature nose of aged cherries and fruits. The body is light and easy to drink, but complex and well structured with acidity pronounced, but also red fruits and delicate earth aspects. The finish is surprisingly quick and clean, leaving the palate generally refreshed.
Grenache, Cab Sauvignon, Tempranillo, Syrah, Carignan

 | 14% | 50€

Clos de l'Obac 2004 opens with a nose holding rich, aged fruits that stack upon each other elegantly. The body is wonderfully balanced, focused and presents an even, elegant wine that, despite the perfection in the elaboration would pair well with no end of dishes.
Grenache, Cab Sauvignon, "Others"

 | 14.5% | 100€

Dolç de l'Obac 2005 is a rich wine for rich foods. The nose isn't sweet like a lesser sweet wine, but well built and while not chocked full of nut aspects, it's bright with red fruits. The body is sweet, but at the same time, it has a good acidity to allow flexibility for dessert pairings as well as others and shouldn't be relegated just to an end of meal pairing.
100% Grenache

 | 16% | 65€/500ml

Alfredo Arribas
owner

GPS
41.167154
0.740541

Clos del Portal

El Molar, *Camí de les Rieres, Mas del Portal*

Visits: By appointment only
Contact: 932531760 | info@portaldelpriorat.com
Website: www.portaldelpriorat.com
Languages: English, French, Italian

Alfredo Arribas is an architect from Barcelona who is quite renowned in Spain and internationally. With countless buildings and publications to his name, in 2001 he took something of an unexpected tangent from his main career and decided to start making wine in the Priorat region. Alfredo considers the DO Montsant and DOQ Priorat appellations as two inseparable sides of the same coin, so he wanted to make wines in both. Although his grandfather had been growing vines in the Ribera de Duero region, he says he came to Priorat with an open mind "free of the ties of tradition" that has allowed him to simply make the wines that the land suggests he makes.

In 2003 he built the winery Clos del Portal alongside the Siurana River in the southern area of the region. On the old Mas del Portal property (where ruins of the old masia still stand up on a hill) Alfredo worked to recuperate 14 hectares of old or abandoned vines as well as plant new ones on terraces. In total, he is working to recuperate 40ha of vineyards to make wine with sooner or later.

In just a few vintages these wines garnered a great deal of well-deserved attention. Afredo, with the technical support of enolog, Joan Asens is working to create a different style of wine that looks towards the future. Overall their wines are fresh on the palate, far less concentrated than what one is used to, but extremely nuanced and absolutely in need of sampling even if the departure from "traditional" Priorat is ultimately too much for some wine drinkers. In that sense Alfredo says his wines are trying to express the character of the land and to connect with the pre-1980s Priorat, rather than the recent big style that had become the norm.

The cellar where they now produce 45,000 bottles a year is compact and focused. Set in to the hill, while very modern in design, it pulls off that wondrous feat of blending in with the natural surroundings by making heavy use of the local llicorella stones for the roof and echoing the curves of the hills.

Gotes 2011 is a very alive and approachable wine that immediately opens up with fruity freshness to the nose and a definitive underlying smokiness. In the body, it easily carries the fresh aspects and adds a good deal of brightness as well. It is undeniably still a Priorat wine, but an understated one.

50% Grenache, 50% Carignan

🔴 | 14% | 13€ | ⚖ | ✦

Negre de Negres 2010 is what Alfredo calls an experimental wine as he uses 5 different clones of Grenache blended with countless other red varieties, thus the name "red of reds". It opens up with a warm embrace of fresh cut roses in the nose, but the minerality is still hanging in the background. It has a wonderfully neutral body that pivots around itself with excellent balance and a smooth, clean, luxurious finish.

60% Grenache, 40% Carignan/Cab Franc/Syrah/Mourvèdre

🔴 | 14% | 22€ | ⚖ | ✦

Somni 2010 is full of cedar and tobacco in the nose, probably due to the new oak barrels used in the aging. This transfers in to a rich, soft body with small touches of minerality, licorice, and mint at the corners of it. The finish pulls up quickly and smoothly, leaving the smallest touch of acidity on the palate.

Carignan, Syrah, Grenache

🔴 | 14% | 34€ | ✦

Tros de Clos 2011 is made from their 100 year-old Carignan vines. Like the others, it's fresh on the palate with the signature minerality at its core. With 14 months in a mix of new and old oak, it's extremely well balanced. The tannic elements don't overpower and it's impossible to find weak points.

100% Carignan

🔴 | 13,5% | 45-48€

CLOS DEL PORTAL

Jordi Vidal
owner & enolog

GPS
41.245216
0.808716

La Conreria d'Escala Dei
Escaladei, *Carrer Mitja Galta, 32*

Visits: Available every day except Sundays at a cost of 10€ per person. Reservations can be made via their website or on the phone. They can also organize tailor-made tastings and meals for a maximum of 35 people.
Contact: 977827055 | laconreria@vinslaconreria.com
Website: www.vinslaconreria.com
Languages: English, French

Down from the Scala Dei Monastery there is a wider area in the valley which historically formed the lands where the non-clergy could live and grow vegetables and animals to eat. A fertile area, it has always been called, "la conreria" and it's here the winery of the same name calls home.

It's a winery started by three friends, an enolog, a priest and a teacher who decided to start making wine while at the wedding of the latter with the grapes from the vineyards owned by the priest. So they started with those seven hectares in 1997 from which they produced 10,000 bottles. In 2000, they planted vines in nearby villages and then in 2004, they planted more in Escaladei. Now, they hold about 27.5ha and produce 80,000 bottles a year. They even have an ambitious project to build a hotel.

They were using another facility up the road before they completed their very modern cellar in 2009. With an eye towards growth down the road, they can fit in more tanks as needed which is important as they keep all the vineyards and varietals separate in the stainless tanks until blending for barrel aging or bottling. Below the main floor, in addition to the various wines aging in a mix of barrels including ones that were specially made for them in Romania, they have the Library. It's an innovative element built in to the cellar wherein people can rent space yearly to age their own wines as they sit alongside those of La Conreria in a controlled environment.

Beyond the various details of their new facilities, co-owner and enolog Jordi Vidal is also an interesting individual in the wine world as he is one of the few people looking towards all aspects of sustainability. More than worrying about how the vineyards affect the surrounding environment, he is also concerned about how the barrels are made and is looking towards ways of reusing the oak barrels longer, not in the name of cost, but in the sole interest of not decimating forests to make barrels that are discarded after only a couple of years use.

Les Brugueres 2011 has a wonderful, pronounced minerality to the nose. It passes easily in to the body and brings up a round quality to the backtaste as well slight citric elements that contribute to a pleasant acidity that carries in to the finish, but cleans out quickly with freshness.
100% White Grenache

 | 14% | 15€

La Conreria 2010 is full of dark fruits and has a brooding quality to it. Tannins come up a bit in the bottle while still transferring the fruits from the nose. A touch of leather and tar grow as well and carry in to the finish. Definitely very food friendly and essentially demands to be paired with a meal.
Grenache, Cab Sauvignon, Merlot, Syrah, Carignan

 | 14,5% | 11€ |

Iugiter 2008 has a nose that initially brings up buttery elements that support the underlying minerality. The body boosts the acidity to balance out the minerality in a nice equalibrium that would still support food pairings, but is at the same time plenty elegant to have on its own. The finish picks up the body elements and lingers pleasantly on the palate.
Grenache, Carignan, Cab Sauvignon

 | 15% | 16.50€

Iugiter Selecció Vinyes Velles 2006 has a nose that is very dark and heavy with the fruits with a touch of vanilla under it. The body is nice and fat but still holds the minerality from the grapes and allows the fruit to come through. Quite luxurious and succulent across the palate with dried herbs and fruits coming across it and fading out to the finish. Not a wine that would allow for much other than cheese pairings, but definitely one to enjoy for an evening.
Grenache, Carignan, Cab Sauvignon

 | 15% | 36€

LA CONRERIA D'ESCALA DEI

José Mas
manager & enolog

GPS
41.16564
0.756784

Costers del Priorat
Bellmunt del Priorat

Visits: Not currently open for public visits
Contact: 618203473 | info@costersdelpriorat.com
Website: www.costersdelpriorat.com

Several friends working in wine who were enamored with Priorat decided to form their own winery in 2002. Most of them had vineyards in Bellmunt, so that's where they decided to produce their wines in a local cellar where they rent space. Their best vineyards are in a gorgeous property with views over the Sarraí mountains, the famous mines of Bellmunt and the cemetery cypresses, from which they take their logo. These are 50-100 year old vines and, unlike the mostly flat vineyards in the southern area near Bellmunt, they are perched out on steep hills with very chunky llicorella soil and unparalleled views of the Ebre River as well as the heavily terraced vineyards of Casa Gran del Siruana across the valley. They also work a vineyard plot in Torroja, bringing the total count of their vineyards to 15 hectares of mainly traditional varieties.

Costers del Priorat had their first vintage in 2003 and have been producing high quality wines ever since with José Mas heading up the enology and management. They are currently producing 45,000 bottles and in time, they hope to establish their own cellar. But for the time being, they're already succeeding quite well in making wines that show the unique locale incredibly well. As José aptly put it, you can replicate a great winery anywhere but you can't replicate a great landscape and vineyards such as these ones.

Old stone terrace

Elios 2010 presents red fruits and spiciness in the nose. Spices pick up in the body as well, and a freshness mixed with the acids becomes prevalent and carries in to the finish. It's relatively light and easy-going overall but with a great character to have with friends and fun meals such as tapas.
55% Grenache, 35% Carignan, 10% Syrah/Cab Sauv

● | 14,5% | 10€ |

Pissares 2010 has a rich, red fruit, and cedar nose upon first opening. The body is initially tight, but opens up to reveal the fruits and acids to make for a good meal wine with a great deal of character to take in. The finish comes up dry and lingers. It is a pleasantly round wine that would pair very well with meals from the grill, including chicken.
55% Carignan, 30% Grenache, 10% Cab Sauv, 5% Syrah

● | 14,5% | 14€

Clos Cypres 2010 is 85% old vine Carignan but will be 100% from 2011 onwards. It needs a good dose of decanting before the elegance of the grapes comes out. Slight red fruits come up in a very subtle and delicate nose that also shows the signature underlying fig aromas. The body is rich and perfectly balanced, showcasing the fantastic tannic and acidic structure of the grapes. It is an incredibly delicious, full-bodied yet completely approachable wine with a refreshing finish.
100% Carignan

● | 14,5% | 25€ | 🏛 | ✺

COSTERS DEL PRIORAT

Cousins Marc and Adrià Pérez have obviously known each other since birth and they've both known winemaking about as long, being members of the influential Pérez family behind Mas Martinet (Adrià is Sara's brother). After being involved in the family wineries and others with friends in DO Montsant, they felt like creating a new project together. So, in 2007 the chance arose to create this new brand when they found an old vineyard in Porrera.

They make all the wine at the Cims de Porrera facilities where they both work and the French names for the wines and project come from their time spent studying in France and working in different chateaus in Bordeaux and Rhône. Their wine labels are based on actual family photos.

L'Antagonique 2011 is a "blanc de noir" in that it's a white wine made from red grapes. The nose starts out with hints of grapefruit and a great big pile of minerality. Light acids come in to the body presenting a tart, lime aspect.

Grenache, Carignan

 | 14% | 11€

Marc Pérez
Adrià Pérez
owners & enologs

Les Cousins
Porrera

Visits: Not currently open for public visits
Contact: 639709133 | adria@lescousins.es / 630886437 | marc@lescousins.es
Website: www.lescousins.es

L'Inconscient 2008 has floral aromas that speak of violets as well as a warm, red fruit nose. The body develops mineral elements quite readily and is very well balanced. The violet elements come back in the finish.
30% Carignan, 25% Grenache, 20% Cab Sauvignon, 15% Merlot, 10% Syrah

● | 15% | 10€ | ⚖ | ✺

La Sagesse 2007 puts out a luscious, dark fruit nose with a touch of vanilla and minerality coming up as well. There is a bright acidity in the body that's juicy and savory with a hint of burnt caramel as well as a touch of coffee both appearing with time. With air, a lemon peel texture comes in to the back of the wine as well. The finish lets the acids linger nicely.
55% Grenache, 45% Carignan

● | 14,5% | 20-25€

Although originally from Torroja, Cristian Francès worked as a jeweler in Barcelona for several years. When his parents retired, they went back to this village of 150 inhabitants looking for peace and quiet. The family had vines since Cristian's great-grandmother's day, but at some point she sold them and Cristian's father decided to buy them again some 15 years ago to sell the grapes off. But with the price of grapes going down and Cristian having landed a job at L'Infernal, learning the winemaking craft, he decided to try his hand at making his own wine in 2003.

He now has a cellar under his house in Torroja and manages to produce about 3,000 bottles. He's looking to grow as each year he plants a few new vines and his next vintage will fully be under the DOQ label, with the cellar hopefully getting certified next year.

Cristian Francés Breton
owner & enolog

Cristian Francés Breton
Torroja del Priorat

Visits: If you visit L'Infernal, most likely you'll meet Cristian and you can ask about his wines. For a taste, Cal Joc in Torroja del Priorat serves by the glass.
Contact: 689321108 | cristian.frances@yahoo.es

Pescallunes 2010 has a very floral nose and a wonderfully fresh body. With air, minerality comes up and makes for a very unique, interesting wine from the region. Only 600 bottles produce a year.
40% White Grenache, 40% Macabeu, 20% Chenin Blanc
🟡 | 14,5% | 12-13€ | |

Rampell 2010 is nicely balanced and rounded. Dark fruits are prevalent throughout all layers of the wine. It's a rare wine in that you can really taste the fruits all the way in through the finish.
80% Grenache, 20% Carignan/Cab Sauvignon
🔴 | 14,5% | 12-14€

Jordi Benito
enolog

GPS
41.129164
1.111424

De Muller
El Molar / Reus, *Mas de les Puces*

Visits: They don't conduct visits at the Priorat cellar, but in Reus they can accommodate groups of 10 to over 200 any day of the week. Weekday visits cost 6€ per person and weekends, 8€ and should be booked in advance by phone or via the form in their website.
Contact: 977756265 | nacional@demuller.es
Website: www.demuller.es
Languages: English

The De Muller Priorat winery is located along the Siurana River in the far south of the DOQ, on the Mas de les Pusses property. There, they have 34 hectares and produce some 200,000 bottles of wine a year, making for one of the biggest producers in the area. There is a great deal of history associated with them as well given that they were one of a handful of wineries to produce bottled wines in Priorat some fifty years ago. But, this cellar is not the one that visitors stop at and it is not much more than a raw production facility for their Priorat wines to be labeled under the DOQ. The other cellar they own is in Reus and it dwarves the Priorat one by leaps and bounds. There, they produce four million bottles a year all under the DO Tarragona label from nearly 200ha of vineyards.

The company was founded by the Tarragona harbor in 1851 by Augusto de Muller and Ruinart de Brimont, from well-known winemaking families of Alsacian origin. Eventually, Augusto ended up in control of the company. Until about 1960 they were an official provider of sacramental wines to the Vatican, which they still produce. For generations the company stayed in the De Muller family, until 1995 when they sold it to the Martorell family. A year later the winery was moved from Tarragona to Reus, where they

Dessert wine aging

had vineyards on the Mas de Valls property. This masia was built in 1405 and they have documents showing that Christopher Columbus visited it prior to his voyage to the New World to observe movements of the sun and earth. The grounds and historic house are immaculately kept, the old wood tanks reach 50,000 liters in capacity, and it's very well suited for large group visits. Of course, it can be a little hard to find off a roundabout from the highway in the direction of the local water treatment plant, but it's definitely worth the trip and a local wine site to behold.

Legitim Criança 2009 has a soft and nicely floral nose. The body is slightly buttery with a good shake of anise, licorice, and fennel elements. The finish is fast and the wine is overall well integrated with itself.

Grenache, Merlot, Carignan, Syrah

● | 14% | 7-8€

Les Pusses 2007 is light in the nose with a touch of plum and lemon peel as well as a minor minerality. The body is slightly tart, but still light and a touch mineral. Overall the body is a direct translation of the nose. As it breathes, acidity comes up and lingers in to the finish.

50% Merlot, 50% Syrah

● | 13,5% | 14-16€

Lo Cabaló Reserva 2006 has a mix of minerality and cedar elements to the nose. The body comes up spicy with a well defined acidity. The minerality drops out in the finish which picks up red fruits. A burnt caramel and light coffee aspect comes in with air

Grenache, Merlot, Syrah, Carignan

● | 14,5% | 19-22€

Josep Roca Benito
owner

GPS
41.192998
0.777682

Devinssi
Gratallops, *Massets 1*

Visits: Available every day for Catalan and Spanish, weekends for English, French and Russian. The cost is 10€ for a cellar visit with a tasting and 15€ including a visit to the vineyards. They can accommodate 2-20 people. Make reservations via their website, Facebook page or phone.
Contact: 977839523, 608892532 | devinssi@il-lia.com
Website: devinssi.com
Languages: English, French, Russian

Josep Roca Benito is an enolog and wine merchant from Barcelona who knew Priorat through selling the wines of Joseph Puig. In 2000 the opportunity arose to buy a nearly abandoned old vineyard in Gratallops and to start recuperating the vines. Three years later he produced his first vintage and in 2005 he bought an old-vine Carignan vineyard with which he makes 300 bottles of his Rocapoll Vi de la Vila.

Focusing solely on producing red wines, Devinssi currently produces nearly 10,000 bottles a year in their small cellar built in what used to be an olive oil mill and modernized by Josep. As he is a man of many trades, he has designed all his wine labels too.

All the wines Josep makes are based on Grenache and Carignan planted on sloped llicorella soils, which give them the typical character of Priorat wines but with his own personal twist. Interestingly, they buck the typical trend of being export driven and sell 80% of their total production locally within Catalonia.

Barrel aging cellar

Cupatge 2009 is a somewhat young wine that they only started making in 2008, and is also their most popular wine. The nose has strong aromas of red fruits with some underlying hints of cocoa. The body is quite fresh overall and light for a younger wine without the strong brashness that you can find in other, more concentrated young wines from the region.

Grenache, Carignan, Cab Sauvignon, Syrah, Merlot

 ● | 14,5% | 7.50€

Mas de les Valls 2009 has its name derived from the intersection of streets where the winery is located in Gratallops. The nose has cherry elements with aromas of raisins and prunes. The body is even and quite mild overall with tannins coming up as well as the Carignan taking over a bit in the profile giving it a deeper quality overall.

Grenache, Carignan, Cab Sauvignon

 ● | 14,5% | 12.50€

Il•lia 2008 is named after an early 10th century noblewoman who lived in Cervera, a town near Priorat. It has a nose with red fruits and a very elegant, balanced quality to it with a touch of fennel. The body is held in good balanced and is very easy to drink, but with a great deal of character and depth. The body is succulent and holds through in to the finish, begging for pairings.

Grenache, Carignan, Cab Sauvignon

● | 14% | 24.50€

Behind a red door on Plaça Catalunya lies the cellar of Domaines Magrez. Despite being in plain sight, you almost wouldn't even realize that it's there if you didn't know where to look. But here, since 2003, they've been producing about 18,000 bottles of wine out of 7 hectares of vineyards. The winery is owned by French winemaker Bernard Magrez and actor, Gerard Depardieu. Magrez owns one of the oldest and most renowned Grand Crus in Bordeaux as well as 34 other estates, located mostly in France, but also in Portugal, Morocco, California, Chile, Argentina, Uruguay, and Spain.

They only make one wine, with Jean-Marc Raynal as the enolog, but consumers will see it under two different labels. The reason for this is that one label features Mister Depardieu prominently and the other doesn't. Given his reputation in France for being "difficult" (drunk driving, drunk flying, tax issues, and most recently gaining Russian citizenship) they decided that not having reference to him on bottles sold in France would be better for business. It's probably a wise choice as nearly all of their production goes to France with only a little being sold locally in Porrera.

GPS
41.187867
0.856643

Domaines Magrez Espagne

Porrera, *Plaça Catalunya, 5*

Visits: Call to make a reservation, but they don't offer them during the harvest.
Contact: 977828016 | trosdelpadri-bernardmagrez@hotmail.com
Website: www.bernard-magrez.com

Herencia del Padrí 2008 has a dark fruit nose with rather mellow minerality. The body is a bit gravelly with larger minerality and stoniness that comes up along with a little fruit and carries in to the finish with a larger punch given by the 18 months in the barrels.
Carignan, Grenache, Merlot, Cab Sauvignon, Syrah

 | 15% | 24€

While it is relatively easy to find Camí de la Solana located just south of El Molar, happening upon Domini de la Cartoixa without the use of a GPS device proves to be a different issue. Down a long winding road that takes you over the rolling hills making up southern Priorat, eventually one comes to a bend in the road surrounded by 70 year-old vines. Here marks the start of the vineyards for the winery.

The solitary Domini de la Cartoixa stands up from the middle of the property the Pérez Dalmau family purchased in 1998. They produced their first vintage in 2001 in a rented space and in 2004 finished their winery. They've been certified as organic from the beginning in all their 11 hectares of vineyards. The owner, Miguel Pérez Cerrada is not only an enolog but also a pharmacist with a PhD in food science and technology. He is extremely passionate about wine and takes great pride in the ones he's making with the advice of consultant Toni Coca. His top wines are named Galena after the lead ore mine in El Molar that closed down in 1975.

It's a well integrated cellar that produces upwards 40,000 bottles. Miguel is more than happy to show visitors about, talk about his passion for wine and have them taste the various wines throughout the aging process.

Miguel Pérez Cerrada
owner

GPS
41.150968
0.719644

Domini de la Cartoixa
El Molar, *Cami de la Solana*

Visits: Available every day at a cost of 5€ per person. Call for reservations.
Contact: 606443736,977771737 | info@closgalena.com
Website: www.closgalena.com

Galena 2008 has dark fruits in the nose, but with a large touch of underlying oak. This carries in to the body a good deal with a small degree of minerality that comes up but is still held at bay by the rather large oak element. The finish comes up dry.
35% Grenache, 25% Cab Sauvignon, 15% Carignan, 25% Merlot
 | 14,8% | 18-20€

Clos Galena 2008 has nose of dark fruits as well as a substantive amount of vanilla from the oak regimen. The body is plush and round with mineral elements that still come through despite the barrels. The finish, while dry still has a decent degree of freshness to it and is pleasing.
40% Grenache, 20% Cab Sauvignon, 20% Carignan, 20% Syrah
● | 14,8% | 30€

Raimon Castellví
owner

GPS
41.189827
0.856139

Celler de l'Encastell
Porrera, *Carrer Castell, 13*

Visits: They welcome 2-12 people at a cost of 8€ per person for a taste and visit to the cellar, although the fee is waived with bottle purchases. Call for a reservation.
Contact: 630941959 | roquers@roquers.com
Website: www.roquers.com
Languages: English

Up above Porrera, there was an old defensive castle that was ultimately destroyed in the Spanish War of Succession about three centuries ago. Despite being little more than a foundation and historical memory, this neighborhood takes its name from the castle and in turn, this winery takes its name from the neighborhood.

For some time the family of Raimon Castellví (whose last name, coincidentally and quiet fantastically, means "wine castle") sold the 75-100 year-old Grenache and Carignan grapes to the local cooperative. But, starting in 1999, they began to make their own wines, bottling their vintages, and ultimately building their cellar that they currently occupy at the top of the village.

Now, they produce 25,000 bottles a year from their eight hectares of vineyards that mix newer and older vines situated up at 400-650 meters, which is considerably higher than the village at 350 meters.

Bottle box

Marge 2010 has a mineral and plum nose. The body is similar, but with acidity that comes up for meals. The finish is spicy and lingers for a bit.

60% Carignan, 35% Cab Sauv, 3% Merlot, 2% Syrah

● | 15% | 14-16€

Roquers de Porerra 2009 has a similar nose, but with more dried herbs to it. The body develops more as well, but pulls back on both ends to be lighter on the palate but with more character with a nice even balance. The finish presents all of the construction of the wine in a nice package, pulling out quickly but with a kick of spiciness to it.

Merlot, Syrah

● | 15% | €

Roquers de Samsò 2010 is 100% Carignan from vineyards of 75-100 years-old. The nose is defined by the larger dark fruits to it that allow a touch of underlying minerality to come through. The body is plush and luxurious, carrying the dark fruits and adding in a little earthiness and root vegetables. The finish is straight shooting and clears out the wine quite well with just a touch of lingering acidity. Only about 500 bottles are made and they're only selling it at the winery.

100% Carignan

● | 15% | 50€ | ✹

CELLER DE L'ENCASTELL

It is quite possible that in the Catalan dictionary if one were to look up "character", Pere Escoda's portrait would be featured prominently. Lively and animated, it is nearly impossible to guess how much time he's been on the planet other than by the amount of stories he has to tell. Everyone who has been around Priorat for awhile seems to have had Pere tending their cellar at some point or another.

Now, Pere just makes his own wine "as a hobby". He proudly declares his winery to be the smallest in Priorat and it might very well be, located in the lower floors of his family home. Of course, it's hard to tell the exact size because as verbose as he is, he's equally meticulous in his cellar with everything in the place it needs to be. He even has a tasting room complete with a collection of wines and spirits from around the world.

Pere makes just 3,000 bottles a year. Almost all of this production he sells to a Spanish restaurant in Sweden minus a couple he keeps for sale locally in Torroja. The arrangement appears to suit him just fine to leave time for traipsing about the two cafés in the village when he's not in the vineyards, which is his favorite place to be.

Pere Escoda
owner & enolog

GPS
41.212464
0.811606

Escoda Palleyá
Torroja del Priorat, *Carrer Font, 16*

Visits: Not currently open for public visits
Contact: 669293283 | perescoda@yahoo.es

Palet 2010 has a dark fruit nose with hints of minerality and walnut initially. The body is light on the palate with a strong acidity that carries the minerality and fruits well. It's a drier style of wine that harks to a somewhat French style, but this changes quickly as it breathes and light cherry, violet, and a beeswax aspect come in to play. Becoming quite floral with time, it finishes quickly and cleanly.
Grenache, Carignan, Syrah, Merlot, Cab Sauvignon

● | 14% | 20€ |  |

Esther Nin
owner & enolog

GPS
41.188154
0.8549

Família Nin-Ortiz

Porrera, *Prat de la Riba, 18*

Visits: Not currently open for public visits
Contact: 686467579 | carlesov@gmail.com

Ester Nin is from Penedès where her family grew vines. She had studied biology and then enology with Sara Pérez and in 2000 she arrived in Priorat to work at Sara's family winery of Mas Martinet. After working at several cellars in the area, in 2004 she became the winery manager at Daphne Glorian's Clos Erasmus in Gratallops and has been there ever since. While producing stellar wines seemingly everywhere she has spent time, she has also been making her own since 2004 and with her partner Carles Ortiz starting in 2008. Ester says that Porrera has something special and is the village she likes the most in Priorat, which is why she ended up making her wines there.

In 1998, Carles purchased a property just south of Porrera in a wonderful valley with an old stone masia next to the creek that runs at the bottom of it. The name of the area is Mas d'en Caçador and there they grow all their vines on the steep slopes that run down the side of the valley. With their mules hanging out by the old house, they're farming in an organic and biodynamic manner. Like many wineries in the region who believe in these methods, but not the paperwork that goes along with them, they're not certified in either at the moment.

Terraced vineyards

While making use of other facilities at the moment, they're quite close to being a full-fledged winery as they have a nice, compact cellar in Porrera with their own tanks and equipment. In total, they're currently producing about 14,000 bottles a year—10,000 of Planetes and 4,000 of Nit de Nin. They're currently aging their wines in 3000L foudres but as of this year they'll start experimenting with clay amphorae. In a year or two they are also planning to start making a white wine with Pedro Ximénez and Macabeu.

Planetes 2010 has a nose that opens with red fruits, founded upon a pleasing base of minerality. The body is light and delicate with floral aspects as well as a small touch of leather. The floral qualities then carry in to a light, soft finish that lingers for some time with gentle, very friendly acidity.

70% Grenache, 30% Carignan

🔴 | 15% | 28€ | ✹

Nit de Nin 2010 is bursting and alive straight out of the glass with boysenberry and other bright, fruits. Rich and fat in the body, it's quite meaty and friendly to the palate. As it decants, the minerality evolves as well as a touch of saltiness. The finish closes up everything quite quickly and posits a very nice, lingering distillate of the wine.

60% Hairy Grenache, 10% Carignan

🔴 | 15% | 55€ | ✹

GPS
41.173954
0.855836

Ferret Bobet

Falset, *Carretera Porrera-Falset, km 6.5*

Visits: Winery visits are free of charge they have a limited availability, mostly during weekdays, so call ahead to make an appointment. They prefer smaller groups and aren't available during the harvest.
Contact: 609945532 | eguerre@ferrerbobet.com, ifortuny@ferrerbobet.com
Website: www.ferrerbobet.com
Languages: English

On the twisty road from Falset to Porrera a futuristic structure lies perched, seeming to hover on the slopes. Those glass panels at the front curve around to provide perfect 180 degree view of the valley from the classy tasting room with Arne Jacobsen-style chairs that looks like the set of Mad Men. The winery building, designed to "operate like a boat stranded among the vineyards" by architects, Miquel Espinet and Antoni Ubach actually looks more like a Star Trek spaceship.

Started in 2002 by friends Sergi Ferrer-Salat and Raül Bobet, the winery looks as if no expense has been spared to make it a showpiece of Priorat. Sergi is a pharmaceutical tycoon with apparently a much greater interest in fine wine than prescription drugs as he is also the owner of famed Monvínic wine bar in Barcelona. His partner Raül was the longtime winemaker at Torres and is also a co-owner of one of the most interesting wineries in Catalonia, Castell d'Encús where stones vats from the 12th century located in the Pyrenees are used to ferment the wines.

Their first vintage was in 2005 and while they produce 25,000 bottles a year, it has all been from grapes that they're carefully selecting from other vineyards in Porrera as well as a smaller amount from El Lloar. Down in the cellar, their range of equipment looks like the wish list of any winemaker and all the grapes pass through large oak bar-

Exterior of the winery

rels, concrete, or stainless steel tanks which work to preserve the quality of the grapes as well as reduce the oak profile in the wines, making for a fresh, bright character in the glass that is only seen in maybe 2-3 other wineries in the region. No expense has been spared to make a wine that is world-class. Typically such ambitions take decades to come to fruition, but Ferrer-Bobet has already had past vintages acclaimed 'Wine of the Year' at home and abroad.

While the winery is impressive, it's the 70 hectares of terraced property around it that are planted with 25ha of vines that are even more striking as they rise up to a peak of 750 meters. They were planted several years ago and farmed in an organic manner, but it was only in 2012 that they harvested their first vintage from them. As time progresses, they hope to be "Carignan pioneers" by making high end, fresh wines made from 100% of those grapes.

Vinyes Velles 2010 has light violet and prune aromas to the nose. Bright and fresh in the body, it balances out a good degree of tannins and acids. Red fruits really come through in the body with an underlying element of the oak present, boosting it. The finish lingers a bit, but fades out with very pleasing fruit left on the palate.
65% Carignan, 34% Grenache, 1% Cab Sauvignon

 | 14,5% | 30€

Selecció Especial 2010 has a delicate nose with touches of dried fig and floral aromas around a core base of roses. The body transitions from the nose quite well and picks up a nice, fresh acidity to it that carries the wine out and through the finish with a hint of tobacco. With time in the glass, more minerality develops and the character deepens.
95% Carignan, 5% Grenache

● | 14,5% | 45€

John Lipscomb
Núria Tobella
owners & enologs

GPS
41.186040
0.772100

Finca Tobella
Gratallops

Visits: Not currently open for public visits
Contact: 686347551 | info@fincatobella.com
Website: www.fincatobella.com

While John Lipscomb was originally an IT expert and Núria Tobella a pharmacist, they met in California while attending the prestigious viticulture & enology program at UC Davis in the early 1990s. They both went on to work at several cellars in Napa Valley such as The Hess Collection, Opus One, Beaulieu Vineyards, and Gloria Ferrer, before coming back to Catalonia a few years later to continue working in the wine industry.

Starting in 2002, John and Núria (along with her family) began buying various parcels of land in Priorat, ultimately ending up with 20 hectares upon which they planted a total of 15ha of vineyards. In addition to their newer vines they planted, they also ended up with a bit more than 1ha of old vines which they blend in to their two reds, except in exceptional growing years where they bottle them separately.

Renting cellar space at a winery in Gratallops to produce their wines, they're one of the few winemakers in Priorat who are striving to make a fresh, "new" style of wine that actually harks back to wines that were produced some 40 years ago. Invigorating in body and approach, they're definitely worth a taste when encountered.

Vines in the infrequent Priorat snow

Negre 2010 opens with a touch of light red fruits and a dusting of minerality underneath. It boasts a good acidity in the body with a large dose of violet and plum tones constant throughout it. As it breathes, it grows a very enjoyable freshness. It's very approachable and food-friendly.

35% Cab Sauv, 25% Syrah, 25% Carignan, 15% Grenache

🔴 | 14% | 10€ | ⚖️

Selecció Especial 2006 initially boasts this soft, stony nose, holding back on the lurking minerality. The body is quite smooth as well. It starts out with a dusty texture to it and a well balanced acidity. As it decants the nose rapidly fills out. The finish is quite fast but it maintains the freshness throughout it. Given enough time, it rounds out really well and develops the smallest touch of earthiness to it.

46% Carignan, 42% Grenache, 12% Cab Sauvignon

🔴 | 14.5% | 18€ | ⚖️ | ✦

Ancients 2009 is produced only from their oldest vineyards of 100+ year old Carignan and 50+ year-old Grenache. The wine is only made in the most optimal of years and is limited to 700 1.5L magnum bottles that are released through auction. The nose opens with a wealth of floral tones and a slight underpinning of sweetness. The body is rich and continues with the bright, complex, and fresh quality seen in their other wines. It's also a bit dusty in texture but sees violet elements poke in from the old Carignan in it, as well as blackcurrant. As it breathes, it stays consistently fresh and pleasant with acidity balanced with downplayed tannins.

79% Carignan, 21% Grenache

🔴 | 14.5% | 120€

Highly regarded French sommelier, Franck Massard decided that after many years "in front of that camera" that he wanted to try his hand in the director's chair and make his own wines.

While there were many threads that came together, the Priorat wines started in 2004 when he bought a vineyard with 20-40 year-old vines on it. Their first vintage was more modest to say the least and yielded a mere 500 bottles.

As the story often goes with winemaking, what started as a hobby has blossomed in to a full-fledged winery that now produces about 20,000 bottles a year and he also has an another label in neighboring Montsant.

Franck Massard
Gratallops

Visits: Not currently open for public visits
Contact: 657298162
Website: www.epicure-wines.com

Humilitat* 2010 shows red berry elements to the nose with a touch of black pepper. A good hit of acids come up in the body to create a wine that's a little spicy, but is generally agreeable overall.
50% Grenache, 40% Carignan
● | 14,5% | 13€

Huellas* 2009 has light touches of dark fruit that lean towards currant with a hint of graphite to the nose. The body initially starts out with large acidity and a bit hot. With air, it cools off a decent amount and gains more balance. The finish shows the acidity and spiciness from the body.
50% Carignan, 40% Grenache, 10% Cab Sauv/Syrah
● | 14,5% | 22€

Jordi Ossó
Ricard Abella
owners

GPS
41.232852
0.845263

Genium
Poboleda, *Carrer Nou, 92*

Visits: Call ahead to book a reservation to visit their cellar and taste their wines. They prefer weekend visits and groups of 4 to 20 people maximum.
Contact: 977827146 | genium@geniumceller.com
Website: www.geniumceller.com
Languages: English

Tucked behind the church that dominates the village of Poboleda is the cellar of Genium, named after a spirit that protected Roman houses. While all roads can somewhat lead there, taking Carrer Major, making a left at the church, and the taking the next right will get visitors to this small, intimate cellar.

For some time, the six families behind Genium had been part of the Poboleda winery cooperative, but in 2002, they banded together to start producing their own wines from the grapes their families had been growing for generations. In 2003 they produced 13,000 bottles of their first vintage. These days they produce eight different wines that total 22,000 bottles. All of them are produced without pesticides or chemicals and one is from certified organic vineyards.

While the winery has been successful and the wines are continually recognized for their high quality, the winery is still something of labor of love for all involved as everyone still works their day jobs (such as a policeman or a civil servant) along with running the winery in a very hands-on family style. They produce about 25,000 bottles of wine from their combined 15 hectares of vineyards.

Roser's 2011 is named after their enologist. It has a fascinating copper color in the glass and a vegetal nose of carrots and turnips as well as fresh elements from the garden. The body good acidity, but remains smooth.
100% Grenache
 | 14% | 10€

Ximenis 2010 sees four months in the barrel. The nose is sweet with a healthy aspect of burnt caramel and presents a very different white from others. It's light across the palate with minerality and an acidity that comes up in the finish while still holding a bit of freshness. Only 1,000 bottles produced each year.
90% Pedro Ximénez, , 10% "Others"
 | 14% | 14€ |

Fresc 2009 has dark berries tinged with a hint of vanilla on the nose. It's light and bright in the body, but still with a good deal of character.

80% Grenache, 20% Carignan

● | 14% | 10€

Celler 2007 has a deep, profound nose with spicy white pepper aspects as it opens. There are large tannins in the body that open in to plush berries. Great equilibrium.

60% Grenache, 20% Carignan, 15% merlot, 5% Syrah

● | 15% | 15€

Celler Ecològic 2007 has a very subtle, delicate nose with gentle, lovely herbs defining the base of it. From start to finish, it holds tannins, acidity, minerality, and all aspects in perfect relation to one another. It's delicious, like a chocolate chip cookie out of the oven.

50% Grenache, 30% Merlot, 10% Carignan, 10% Syrah

● | 14,5% | 17.50€ | ✹

Poboleda 2008 has stronger berry elements in the nose and shows minerality with air. The tannins drift in to a soft, plush body that's lovely across the palate. The finish pulls out well with a touch of red fruits.

70% Grenache, 20% Carignan, 10% Merlot

● | 15% | 17.50€ |

Costers 2008 shows a nose is rich with layers of crème to it. It's smooth, luscious, and balanced with all of its aspects working with one another to stick on the palate and leave only the best elements of the wine.

50% Carignan, 30% Grenache, 10% Merlot, 10% Syrah

● | 15,5% | 27€

Excel•lent 2007 is a "peak year" wine. There are hints of chocolate and granitic elements that come through in the nose. While slightly plush and bright, it still speaks wonderfully well of the grapes that went in to it.

60% Carignan, 30% Grenache, 10% Syrah

● | 14,5% | 30€ | ✹

Josep Àngel Mestre
manager & enolog

GPS
41.16566
0.767152

Gran Clos
Bellmunt del Priorat, *Carrer Montsant, 2*

Visits: Not currently open for public visits
Contact: 977830675,629886398 | josepa@granclos.com
Website: www.granclos.com

Near the end of the village of Bellmunt, Gran Clos was started in 1995 by Josep Maria Fuentes who made his first vintage that same year. With the recuperation of old vines in the area, their initial production of just 5,000 bottles a year increased to 25,000 by 1999. In 2000, Falset native, Josep Ángel Mestre took over the enology duties and they continued to expand, producing high quality wines from the area that were a mix of their grapes as well as some bought from others. In 2004, Irish businessman and long time wine lover John Hunt bought the winery. He's also the owner of the Oriel Wines brand, who finds top winemakers in the best wine regions around the world, has them make wines with top quality grapes, and sells them to website members under one simple name.

Currently Gran Clos lays claim to 30 hectares and produces about 60,000 bottles a year made solely from their own vineyards. As is typical, they export the vast majority of the wines they produce outside of Spain. Their cellar is best summed up as "functional". It doesn't have the grandness that others in the region have, but it does what Josep Ángel needs to make the wines that he feels best represent the Priorat landscape and that he's happy with. This is especially true given that he's seen how the bottles hold up over a decade under his steady hand. The Gran Clos was considered to be the best wine of Priorat in a blind tasting held some years ago comparing all the best wines produced over a decade in the region.

Gran Clos Blanc 2004 has a nose with slight petrol elements and bitter citrus. Bright and citric in the mouth, it's refreshing while at the same time full of body. The aromas of the nose transfer a good deal in to the body making for a different white for the region, especially with the aging regimen.
50% White Grenache, 50% Macabeu

 | 14,5% | 12€ |

Les Mines (Solluna) 2009 has two names depending on the destination country, but is otherwise the same wine. The nose shows a decent degree of minerality with an underlying blend of red and dark fruits with a hint of syrup qualities just on the fringe. The body brings up acidity and tannins in equilibrium with a balanced aspect to it that's bright, fresh, and able to be paired with many dishes.
70% Grenache, 20% Carignan, 10% Merlot

 | 14% | 12€

Finca el Puig 2004 has a complex nose of red fruits with herbal wild elements like touches of sage. The body perfectly picks up on all of these elements as well as grabbing a larger, enjoyable dose of anis and licorice.
50% Grenache, 10% Carignan, 20% Syrah, 20% Cab Sauvignon

 | 15% | 18€

Gran Clos 2005 carries wondrous dark fruits throughout its nose with slight underpinnings of vanilla and prune with a steady foundation of earthiness. The body is balanced with acids, but brings up a good deal of herbaceous elements as well. Succulent and deep, it keeps changing a great deal as it breathes, letting out different earthy aspects.
55% Grenache, 30% Carignan, 15% Cab Sauvignon

 | 15,5% | 35-40€ | ✹

Cartus 2005 is a special selection of 100 year-old vines. It has a nose fresh with olive oil and butter as well as leather aspects and definitive wild herb aspects. The elements from the nose transfer well in to the body and set up stronger herbal and olive oil components. On top of this, fresh acids float while the wine remains quite deep overall. The finish comes up drier than others, but carries the herbal elements with a grand elegance that makes it a wine to enjoy by itself as opposed to pairing it with a meal.
74% Grenache, 26% Carignan

 | 15% | 80-100€ | ✹

GRAN CLOS

Jordi Fernández
manager & enolog

GPS
41.212521
0.760297

Gratavinum
Gratallops, *Mas d'en Serres*

Visits: They're available any day including holidays. Call for reservations or make one via their website. During the olive picking and pressing season they also offer tours of their oil-making facilities.
Contact: 938901399 | gratavinum@gratavinum.com
Website: www.gratavinum.com
Languages: English

The Cusiné family had been attracted to the wild and rugged landscape of Priorat for years, but the opportunity to start a winery in the region ultimately arose in 2003. They have been producing wines in Penedès for three generations at the Parés Baltà winery, located in an area where vines where originally planted in 1790. Since they knew René Barbier III, it was only natural that they would end up purchasing old vines near those of Clos Mogador, a bit past Álvaro Palacios' winery.

Perched out of the steep hills of Gratallops, the view from the vineyards is one of those rare ones that allows the visitor to take in a great panorama of Priorat. Having farmed their vineyards in Penedès organically for years, they also applied organic agriculture to their Priorat vineyards from the start. In 2012 they started the process to gain biodynamic certification as well and started using only natural yeasts. They're also one of the few wineries that only dry farms all their vineyards, using no irrigation other than what falls from the sky. The purpose being that it forces the vines to grow their roots deeper and produce more intensely flavorful grapes. It's easier to do with old vines, but they apply this to their younger vines planted in 2004 as well. Their enolog, Jordi Fernández says that at the base of the winery's philosophy is respecting the grape's natural growth.

Olive oil pressing

Their grapes come from their nine hectares, as well as three additional hectares they source from and produce about 25,000 bottles a year. Their cellar is in a curious location as you actually have to pass through La Vilella Baixa on a road next to an interesting-looking old watermill to get there. But it's there that they have their compact, productive winery as well as their olive oil press.

It's quite important to note that they are only one of two independent olive oil makers in all of Priorat, as most of the production is done by the cooperatives. What they produce is unadulterated, brilliant oil that literally shimmers like gold when you look at it straight out of the press. Naturally, the flavor is of as high a quality as their wines.

As of 2011 they started making a limited-edition fully natural wine called, Silvestris that they haven't released yet.

2piR 2008 has a nose of red fruits and a touch of fennel and other herbs from the vineyard. It's strong in the body but quite balanced overall with a good deal of character that pulls through right in to the finish that lingers a bit. It is aged for 12 months in a mix of French and Hungarian oak.
60% Grenache, 25% Carignan, 15% Cab Sauv/Syrah
 | 14,5% | 20€

GV5 2008 starts out with a nose of dark fruits with a hint of violet from the old Carignan and a nice, rounded minerality as the foundation. It's nice and fresh in the body with a clean elegance that shows off the minerality very well in to the bright, wonderful finish that hints at a slightly buttery texture just at the end. It's aged for 10 months.
77% Carignan, 15% Grenache, 8% Syrah
● | 14,5% | 40€ | ✹

Started in 2000, Heid & Marqués is located directly under Cal Joc restaurant in Torroja, in a building that has existed as a cellar since 1883. Now remodelled and with modern facilities, the cellar currently produces about 10,000 bottles annually.

It's a modern, compact cellar that was founded by Josep Maria Marqués and Ferran Torra, the latter of which is the father of the Rotllan Torra brothers whose winery of the same name is in Torroja. Moreover, Heid & Marqués is run by another Torroja winemaker, Pere Escoda. While they produce a good number of bottles, they don't actually own any vineyards and buy all their grapes from others in the area. All their wines are aged for at least 14 months in French and American oak barrels.

Pere Escoda
manager

GPS
41.212807
0.809726

Heid & Marques
Torroja del Priorat, *Carrer Nou ,92 baixos*

Visits: Call for a reservation or make one through their website.
Contact: 934734844,616981938 | info@heidmarques.com
Website: heidmarques.com

Collita 2010 has a mineral and dark plum nose while it is quite large in the body. A good deal of graphite aspects come up, but it is overall quite throaty and coarse.
100% Grenache

🔴 | 15% | 9-10€

Reserva 2006 has boysenberry and dark fruits on the nose. It's quite strong with barrel aromas and flavors. It levels out a little with a good degree of decanting, but is overly robust and non-integrated.
Grenache, Carignan, Merlot

🔴 | 15% | 14-16€

Manuel Hidalgo
owner

GPS
41.24299
0.831704

Hidalgo Albert

Poboleda, *Carretera Poboleda-Escaladei, km 8*

Visits: A maximum of 12 people can have a visit of the cellar and taste of the wines for 12€ a person. Call for reservations.
Contact: 659060692,977842064 | hialmi@yahoo.es
Website: www.cellerhidalgoalbert.com
Languages: English

Going west from Poboleda in the direction of Escaladei, there is a bend in the road where a dirt path veers off and up alongside the mountains. It's this turn (which is often parked in by mushroom and boar hunters depending on the season) that leads up and around to Hidalgo Albert. Once you reach the winery, you can see that it's not actually that far from the main road, but is tucked away in a small recess of the hills in an area known by the locals as Les Salanques.

It was there that Manolo Hidalgo purchased his third property with the idea of building a cellar in the old stone masia. The first two properties he bought between 2003 and 2004 were el Barranc del Coll Beix and Matxerri. In the following years he built terraces and planted vines with his wife Josefina (whose last name Albert is the other half of the winery name). Manolo has been in the wine business for 26 years, working in sales and distribution, but the winery is a labor of love in which all family members have been participating. They made their first vintage in 2007, under the guidance of well-known enolog Toni Coca.

Their vineyards are 50% Grenache, 15% Carignan, with the rest made up of Syrah, Cabernet Sauvignon, Cabernet Franc, and Merlot. For barrels, they use a mix of 85% French and 15% American oaks. Currently, they're producing about 25,000 bottles a year but once they finish their initial winery project they will be able to produce more than 100,000. All their production is organic.

They've built the winery with visitors in mind and set up several nice areas to taste their wines both inside the cellar as well as up top alongside the vineyards for those warmer summer days.

1270 A Vuit Blanc 2011 has a nose that comes up with neutral aromas drifting in to minerality with the smallest hints of citrus. In the body, it's very round and surprisingly chewy and tasty. The finish is initially rich, but cleans out quickly in a refreshing manner. It's a very satisfying wine overall with a maximum production of 800 bottles. It is fermented in oak barrels and aged in them for 5 months. The name is a reference to the foundation of Poboleda.
100% White Grenache

 | 15% | 11-13€ |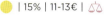

Fina 2010 is named after Manuel's wife. It opens fresh in the nose with hints of apricot. In the body, it's quite simple overall and while not complex, is a good pairing for meals and general drinking. As it opens, more fig and prune elements come up mixed with a touch of the signature minerality of the region. It is aged in oak barrels for 12 months.
50% Grenache, 30% Syrah, 10% Merlot, 10% Cab Sauvignon

 | 14,5% | 10-12€ |

1270 A Vuit Negre 2009 brings up more cherry elements in to the nose that carry in to the body. A sweeter construction overall, it still allows for acids to come up and in to the finish for a very proper meal wine. It could probably stand for another year or so in the bottle to reach its full character as shown when tasted against previous vintages. It is aged in oak barrels for 14 months.
40% Grenache, 20% Syrah, 20% Cabernet Sauv, 10% Merlot, 10% Carignan

 | 15% | 18-22€

Pep Aguilar Foz
manager & enolog

GPS
41.213844
0.817048

L'Infernal
Torroja del Priorat, *Finca de l'Hort Tancat parcela 148*

Visits: Available on a limited basis, call for details and reservations.
Contact: 977828057, 600753840 | yalellamaremos@yahoo.es
Website: www.trioinfernal.es
Languages: English, French

This project in Priorat was born in 2002 by three winemaker friends from three different appellations in the Rhône Valley: Laurent Combier, Peter Fisher, and Jean-Michel Gerin. They had known each other for decades through the Rhône Vignobles association and decided to join forces for this new venture. In 2001, they were aided a good deal by René Barbier who helped them find the land they purchased which is a mix of rugged old vines from 1912 as well as new ones that they planted in 2002. For those who might look out from the top of Torroja and wonder which vines are theirs, just scan the hills for "Trio Infernal" written large with bushes.

In 2002, Pep Aguilar and Cristian Francés both joined the project as the local enologists to take care of the day to day work in the cellar and vineyards. Trio Infernal has a 14 hectare vineyard between Torroja and Gratallops, and eight hectares of old vineyards in Torroja that run at a slope of 70% which makes for a hair-raising drive up the side on the switchback trails. It also makes for a lot of hand work as machines simply can't work on that steep of a grade.

Their first harvest to be made in their own, modern cellar was in 2012 and they typically produce between 25-30,000 bottles a year although 2012 saw a smaller production as it was a very low-yield year. To make their white wine, they purchase grapes from growers in La Vilella.

0/3 2011 is aged for 14 months. It presents a beautiful golden color and a neutral nose and body that are both well balanced. There is an underlying minerality that blends in with a honey aspect and white fruits. A generally summery character, a fresh, citric bitterness develops as well as sweet lychee.
White Grenache, Macabeu

 | 14% | 20€

Riu 2010 opens with a nose that has a blend of minerality, lighter amounts of dark fruits, and ripe cherries. The body is soft on the palate with a good degree of acidity mixed with a dose of the minerality that comes through from the nose. It's quite approachable and easy to drink overall, but lacks a bit of depth so it would pair well with meals.
Carignan, Grenache, Syrah

 | 14,5% | 17€

1/3 2006 has an initial hit of mineral and dark fruits to the nose with an underlying blackcurrant. The body is large and mineral, coming across as a bit hot at first. Some stewed tomato aspects come up as well as chewiness that sticks in the wine along in to the finish.
Grenache, Carignan

● | 14,8% | 30€

2/3 2007 has a dark berry nose with hints of vanilla that are well integrated with the mineral elements. The well formed tannins make a plush palate, along with the dark fruits that continue to carry along in to the finish. It is fluid wine that knows where it's going. As it decants, it develops a pleasing dustiness. Despite the general size of the wine, it would be great for spicy foods.
100% Carignan

● | 14,8% | 55€

L'INFERNAL

Jaume Mas
enolog

GPS
41.270116
0.870205

Joan Ametller
La Morera de Montsant, *Finca Mas del Mustardo*

Visits: They primarily hold visits on Thursdays that include visiting the cellar, vineyards, and tasting three wines for 9€. Call ahead to reserve or to see if other days are available.
Contact: 933208439,690823650 | ametller@ametller.com
Website: www.ametller.com
Languages: French

There is a road from La Morera to Cornudella that skirts along the edge of the Montsant bluffs. It's a staggering view to take in with the mountains on one side and a nearly aerial vantage of the entire Priorat on the other. It's really a wonder there aren't more accidents, but here, nearly tucked against the edge of the mountain is the Joan Ametller winery.

They started making their wines in 2002, built their winery in 2003, and had their first full harvest there in 2004. The owner, Joan Ametller Civill is originally from Penedès and is from a long line of winemakers going back seven generations to 1824. Like most that come to Priorat, he found great potential in the unique soils of the area and decided to establish a winery there, adding to a large family portfolio of winemaking.

Their properties are quite varied with the 20 hectares they have up in La Morera mainly on sandstone and clay soils where the winery is based and then another five hectares down in Porrera on llicorella soils. All told they're able to produce about 90,000 bottles a year of red and white wines and even one of the rare rosés made in Priorat.

Clos Corriol Rosat 2012 has very aromatic nose full of raspberries and red currants, as well as a touch of sweetness that translates in to a similar body. The finish comes up fresh and clean overall. It is a good wine to pair with creamy cheeses.
Cab Sauvignon, Grenache
 | 13% | 6€

Clos Corriol Blanc 2012 has a nose that is citric and floral. Light in the mouth, it has a touch of orange blossom to the body. Clean in the finish, it's a simple, but overall enjoyable and refreshing wine.
100% White Grenache
 | 13,5% | 7€

Clos Mustardó Blanc 2009 has a nose that's light with slight citric elements and touches of lemon peel. The body is fresh, but decently tannic and has a soft cantaloupe aspect to it that makes it rather round on the palate. This roundness carries in to the fresh finish.

White Grenache, Macabeu, Pedro Ximénez

 | 14% | 10€

Clos Corriol Negre 2009 has touches of dark cherry and licorice in the nose. The body is dry and a bit tannic, but generally favorable and set up well to pair with meals. The minerality comes up a tiny bit in the finish, but in general, it maintains the young, dark cherry elements throughout.

Grenache, Carignan

 | 14% | 8€

Clos Mustardó Negre 2006 has a nose with some red fruits, but also a touch of prune and dark fruits. The body has a good balance of acidity, tannins and a touch of the dark fruits that would make it pair wonderfully with strong, hard cheeses like Parmesan or Stilton. It carries similar aspects into the finish. Very consistent overall but has aged cherry aspects that may not speak to some drinkers.

Grenache, Merlot, Cab Sauvignon

● | 14% | 11€

Els Igols 2004 spends at least 12 months in oak depending on the year. The nose has hints of vanilla and slight herbal elements although it's generally quite subtle overall. The body has stronger tannins than their other wines with a larger aspect of leather to it. Slight undertones of coffee come up as well that lead in to a fast, easy finish. While generally robust, it comes across quite light and easy to drink overall.

Merlot, Grenache, Carignan, Cab Sauvignon

 | 14% | 20€

Gerard Batllevell Simó
owner

GPS
41.188174
0.856306

Joan Simó

Porrera, *Carrer de Onze de Setembre, 7*

Visits: They're available every day at a cost of 10€. Call for a reservation.
Contact: 977830993,627563713 | leseres@cellerjoansimo.com
Website: www.cellerjoansimo.com
Languages: English

Alongside the Cortiella river that flows through Porrera and the old bridge that crosses it, you'll find the Joan Simó cellar. Started by Gerard Batllevell Simó, it's named after his maternal grandfather who was a grower that sold his grapes to the Gratallops collective. Gerard wanted to start making use of the old family vineyards to produce his own wines instead of just selling them off and his enolog friend Josep Ángel Mestres of Gran Clos joined him in the task to start with a production of 1,000 bottles in 1999. Where the cellar sits now was used as firewood storage as well as a stable for animals that has now been turned into a modern winemaking facility. The cellar is appropriately "cellar-y" with barrels stacked up to the vaulted ceilings and along the old brick walls. There's even a "secret" bottle aging room that's tucked in to what appears to be an old water mine below the main tank room.

Over time, between the old vineyards and what's been planted anew, they harvest from 15 hectares of vineyards spread across five different properties on the 150 mountainous hectares that the family owns. Since they have some vineyards in Porrera and others in Bellmunt and these two areas have quite different climates, their harvest spans nearly two months. Their production is currently about 20,000 bottles a year that they mostly export.

In the cellar

Sentius 2007 opens with mineral qualities to the nose and a buttery aspect at the bottom of it. The body is initially rather large and earthy in texture. It's bright with red fruits, plums, and acidity that pulls the wine in to the finish.

48% Grenache, 15% Merlot, 15% Cab Sauvignon, 12% Syrah, 10% Carignan

🔴 | 15% | 15€

Les Eres Vinyes Velles 2008 is produced from their old vine Grenache and Carignan. It tosses out a warm, red fruit nose initially with a touch of kiwi and minerality coming up quickly as it breathes. There's a good degree of acidity to the body as well as an underlying dustiness. While plush, the minerality pulls on this aspect a great deal and create a dry texture overall. The buoyant acidity runs straight through in to the lingering finish.

55% Grenache, 30% Carignan, 15% Cab Sauvignon

🔴 | 15% | 35€ | ✺

Les Eres Especial dels Carners 2007 is a single-estate limited edition Vi de Guarda of only 300-600 bottles per year produced from their oldest vineyard. It has a nose immediately opening with mineral aspects, but is light and balanced, like fresh rain. The body is rich with red fruits as well as mineral and chewy with a delicious texture overall. As it breathes, it develops soft, floral aromas. It remains balanced and with a gracious equilibrium on the palate and shows a perfectly made wine. The finish brings up hints of the acidity and minerality lingering past the back taste.

75% Grenache, 25% Carignan

🔴 | 15,5% | 90€ | ✺

JOAN SIMÓ

While Paco Rivero has a shipping business Barcelona, he's found a great deal of passion and solace in his vineyards. He came to Priorat for the first time in the 1990s with his wife Rosa García and they liked it so much they bought a weekend house in La Vilella Baixa. Being a wine lover for as far as he can remember and having a house in Priorat, it was inevitable that he would end up making wine. It all started in 2004 when he took a course at the Catalan Wine Institute in viticulture. Then he bought a few vines in el Lloar in 2006, then a few more, and eventually he produced his first vintage in 2007.

Currently Paco works with two small vineyards in El Lloar and Gratallops and he takes care of the vines personally with great satisfaction. Thanks to a personal connection to Pau Mur, he's been making his wines at the Sabaté i Mur winery in Torroja where enolog Jordi Sabaté advises him on the more technical aspects. His overall production is quite small at only about 3,000 bottles a year which he finds to be a good amount. In 2013, though, he has established his own cellar in La Vilella Baixa and will hopefully produce his next vintage there. Also, in 2012 he planted a new vineyard with White Grenache to start making a white wine soon.

Paco Rivero
owner

GPS
41.218412
0.76378

Lo
La Vilella Baixa, *Carrer Catalunya 25*

Visits: Not currently open for public visits
Contact: 630196138 | info@celler-lo.com
Website: www.celler-lo.com
Languages: English

Jove 2010 is a pleasantly surprising young wine. Overall it's balanced and keeps its fruits under control as opposed to how a young wine can quickly get out of hand. While still fruity in the body, it brings up acidity well to potentially play nicely with many dishes.
100% Grenache

🔴 | 14% | 9€ |

Lo Temps 2008 has a dark fruit nose that's smooth with violet and herbal notes. The body starts out fresh, but ends up presenting mineral and herbal elements at the end. The acidity is well defined along with notes of cocoa and roasted nuts that come out with air.
70% Grenache, 15% Carignan, 15% Cab Sauvignon

🔴 | 15,3% | 18€

Maria Arnal
owner

GPS
41.213743
0.811993

Llicorella Vins
Torroja del Priorat, *Carrer de l'Era, 11*

Visits: They cost 5€ a person for a visit and tasting. Reservations should be made two days in advance.
Contact: 619542330,977211471 | comercial@llicorellavins.com
Website: www.llicorellavins.com

Situated at the end of Torroja next to the local bus stop, the cellar of Llicorella Vins is truly a family project that's located on the ground floor of the old Cal Farré home. The Arnal siblings take care of all aspects of running the winery: Josep is the enolog, Guillem is the owner of the vineyards andtakes care of them, Carme designs the labels and brochures, Eduard handles the accounting, and Maria does a little bit of everything such as visits and sales. Although their grandfather had already made wine in Tarragona and Penedès, they started the winery in 2000 in partnership with the Milà brothers. They made their first vintage of Mas Saura in 2001.

The Mas de Saura property is an old holding in the area that's situated at 350 meters in altitude with eleven hectares of vineyards. While old Carignan vines had been planted there in the 1940's, it wasn't until 1993 that they began a recuperation of them as well as planting new vines of Grenache, Cabernet Sauvignon, and Syrah.

In their compact cellar under the family house, they've been focused on making wines for aging. For instance, they haven't ever made any young wines and stick to more full bodied, deeper wines that are all from their own vineyards. They currently produce about 10,000 bottles with their estate grapes.

Cellar exterior

Aònia 2010 has a nose of dark fruits and hints of fig. The body carries these aromas well and picks up acidity and tannins to round out the wine to fill up the palate. It transitions well to the finish and is fresh all around.
Grenache, Carignan, Cab Sauvignon

 | 14,8% | 9-11€

Gran Nasard 2008 has a mix of red and dark fruits to the nose with a more pronounced minerality. The body is quite plush and velvety in the mouth and will increase with these textures as it ages. Herbal elements are more pronounced in the flavors and there is a good equilibrium to the wine overall as it pulls out in to an easygoing, smooth in a classic style.
Grenache, Carignan

 | 14,5% | 14-15€

Mas Saura 2003 has a very sophisticated dark fruit nose with herbal elements flowing freely throughout it. The body is wonderful and luscious, filling out the palate in herbal elements from the field as well as definitive minerality that carries in to a rich, full finish. The 2005 and 2008 vintages are still climbing towards their most optimal moment to shine.
Grenache, Cab Sauvignon, Syrah

 | 14,5% | 22-25€ |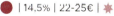

750 Anys de Torroja de Priorat is a wine made for the 750th anniversary of the founding of Torroja that blended a little bit of wine from all the cellars in the village in 2011. The nose is a bit mixed, but shows the general slate and mineral qualities found in the area. The body is initially a bit tight, but carries the aromatic elements well and expands on the minerality as well as adding in a smoother, buttery element that carries in to the finish. A generally fine wine overall, but definitely a difficult blending to make from 10 separate cellars without any count as to what percentage of what grapes went in to it.

● | 14,5% | 15€

Maius is accessed via the road that goes in the direction of Cornudella from the south. Turning left off the main road and driving for three kilometers down this somewhat bumpy dirt road you eventually come to the terraces of the winery, just across from the Mongolian yurts that some French set up to use for retreats and summer camps.

It was back in 1949 that the Gómez family opened a shop in Sant Cugat del Vallès selling bulk wines. They changed things up in 1992 to serve food and specialize heavily in local products. This love of the locale eventually led Josep Gómez Puig (the son of the original founder) to start his own winery in Priorat in 1998 with the family of well-known enolog Joan Milà from Penedès. They had their first vintage release in 2004 and their enolog is Joan's son Eloi.

While the terraces are sharp and carved in to the earth with a mix of 7-8 year-old vines as well as few older vines, the structure for the winery is largely unseen. They worked to build 85% of it underground to remove the need to cool it during summer and rely on solar energy. Currently, they have 7ha planted on the 22 that make up the property which they are starting to certify as organic.

Josep Gómez Puig
owner

GPS
41.244684
0.879973

Maius
La Morera de Montsant, *Barranc de la Bruixa, km 3*

Visits: It's free to visit the winery with a maximum of eight or so people. Call to make a registration.
Contact: 696998575 | jgomez@maiusviticultors.com
Website: www.maiusviticultors.com
Languages: English, Russian, Romanian

Negre Assemblage 2009 is a semi-criança starts out with tobacco aspects mixed with small amounts of minerality and fig to the nose. This translates in to the body where the tobacco grows a great deal and even carries in to the finish. As it decants, a petrol hint comes up at the very end of the finish as well.
65% Grenache, 20% Carignan, 15% Cab Sauvignon

● | 14,5% | 11-12€

Negre 2010 has bright, red fruits in the nose that develop a chocolate undertone as it breathes. The body is surprisingly fresh and open, welcoming easy drinking. Tannins and depth are largely downplayed as acids come up to make for healthy food pairings as well as approachability by most anyone.
45% Grenache, 30% Carignan, 25% Cab Sauvignon

● | 14,5% | 14-15€

David Marco
Olivia Bayés
owners

GPS
41.195378
0.858542

Marco Abella

Porrera, *Carretera Porrera-Cordunella, km 1.3*

Visits: Reserving ahead by email or phone, visitors can have a visit of the vineyard, winery, and cellar, followed by a tasting for 15€ that takes about two hours. Minimum of three people and a maximum of 25.
Contact: 933712407, 977262825 | info@marcoabella.com
Website: www.marcoabella.com
Languages: English

Just outside of Porrera, past the 1km marker on the road to Cornudella sits the modern winery, Marco Abella. Perched amongst their swooping terraces, it embodies a family journey in wine that began some 500 years ago. From this time there exist records of the Marco family being in Porrera. They were working these sharp, unyielding lands of the Priorat for generations, until phylloxera hit and decimated the entire region. At that time, the grandfather of David Marco went to Barcelona in search of better fortunes, found them, and stayed.

It took two generations, but David and his wife, Olivia Bayés decided that they wanted to change the path of their Barcelona lives as a telecommunications engineer and a lawyer, move to Priorat and restart the family wine business. There are many who have romantic ideas of making this happen, but these people aren't aware of the effort needed. David and Olivia were and have put in hard hours making the winery that exists there come to be, and to produce excellent wines.

In 1999, they started recuperating the old family vines and also growing new ones. After the good results of their first vintage in 2004 they produced in a rented space, in 2005 they started building their modern cellar on the property designed by David's sister, Eva Marco. They focused on making it a fully gravity fed system so that no pumping was needed during wine production. They incorporated other methods in to their winemaking that aren't commonly seen like cryomaceration of the grapes, leaving them in cold storage for 10 hours after picking as well as making heavy use of concrete aging tanks instead of stainless steel or oak and they only use natural, local yeasts.

From 23 hectares of organic vineyards they currently produce around 50,000 bottles a year with labels designed by renowned Catalan painter Josep Guinovart.

Òlbia 2009 is limited production of only 600 bottles. They only made in the most optimal years which is the reason it has such a limited release. The nose shows off fuzzy aromas with a texture of cantaloupe. The body is very interesting with a touch of oak and hazelnuts. It has an initial aroma of rose and lychee. The aromas translate well in to the body to make for a balance wine. The finish brings up a hint of mandarin with air.
80% Macabeu, 20% White Grenache

 | 13.5% | 26-28€ |

Loidana 2008 is a woman's name from the Middle Ages. The wine is designed to be soft, fruity and easy to drink. Initially it has a mineral nose that then blows off to reveal small dark berry elements and a touch of acidity that comes up more in the body. Fresh in the body it softens up on the palate as it breathes but manages to maintain acidity well.
50% Grenache, 30% Carignan, 20% Syrah, 10% Cab Sauvignon

 | 14.5% | 10-11€ | ⚖ |

Mas Mallola 2008 has a fruity, rich nose of dust and other light mineral aspects with a touch of licorice. It's light across the palate, but not the least bit weak in body with a nice balance of acidity, tannins, and elegance. The finish pulls out in a very light fashion that matches the body.
55% Grenache, 40% Carignan, 5% Cab Sauvignon

 | 14.5% | 17-19€

Clos Abella 2005 spends 24 months in French oak and two years in the bottle before selling. It has a luscious dark fruit nose that's silky and luxurious. It's fat on the palate, but not heavy and large. The balance holds through really well in to the perfect finish.
55% Grenache, 40% Carignan, 5% Cab Sauv/Syrah

● | 14.5% | 35-38€

Diane Pitsch
Bixente Oçafrain
managers

GPS
41.221947
0.774094

Mas Alta
La Vilella Alta, *Carretera La Vilella Baixa-Poboleda, km 1*

Visits: Available with prior reservation by phone.
Contact: 977054151, 977817194 | info@bodegasmasalta.com
Website: www.bodegasmasalta.com
Languages: English, French, German, Dutch

If driving around the western side of Priorat, it's impossible not to notice the Mas Alta winery on the road between Gratallops and La Vilella Alta. Started in 1999 by six Belgian partners, they produced their first vintage in 2004. Mas Alta is quite a striking winery and reminiscent of the French chateaux, although the steep mountains and terraces around it give a distinctly Priorat feel to it. It should be noted that inside, the chateau is a bit of a work in progress as they continue to build out the sections above the cellar.

Technically, they have an impressive, gravity-fed modern cellar including concrete tanks for some of the initial fermentation of the wine and a nice cellar chocked full of French oak barrels for final aging. All of this allows them to make wines that they feel are their expression of the locale. The vineyards and lands outside the cellar from where the grapes come from are quite fascinating and that's where they concentrate their efforts. They have some old terraces that are banked with the local slate stones and still have the hovering stone steps that people used to pass from one terrace to the next.

Naturally, there are other vineyards as well that they rent and maintain. Some of these are up to 90 years old and provide them with their most robust grapes. All told, they have 30 hectares of their own as well as the five ha that they rent, spread out over a rather crazy total of 40 different small properties. Once they harvest everything, they produce some 80,000 bottles a year which is overseen by enolog consultants Michel Tardieu and Philippe Cambie from France and managed daily by the dedicated and incredibly amiable three person team based in Priorat.

The wines of Mas Alta are overall a very different style than other wines found in the region. They drift in to a sweeter aspect with more floral elements. It may be a welcome change for some and a wine that may drift too far from what Priorat "should" be for others.

Artiga Blanc 2011 has a pleasantly complex nose with hints of lemon peel. This comes in to the body and it boasts large acids that remain in control and give a citric quality to the body that carries in to the finish.

White Grenache, Macabeu, Pedro Ximénez

 | 14,5% | 25-28€

Artigas Negre 2008 is from a mix of 90 year-old Carignan vines as newer Grenache and Cabernet Sauvignon. It has a mineral nose with dark berries that's more stony than plush. The body comes up sweeter than most of this level and the sweetness sticks strongly in to the finish with some violet notes.

70% Grenache, 25% Carignan, 5% Cab Sauvignon

 | 14,5% | 19€

La Basseta 2010 has a nose full of slate aromas, slight dark fruits, and a touch of dark cherry. The body is large, but generally fresh and crisp overall. The slate elements come up more and give it a large boost. The finish picks up on the tannins and lingers well. About 30% of the grapes in the blend has been fermented with their stems.

100% Grenache

 | 14,5% | 59€

Old stone terraces

Josep Alfons Cazurra Basté is the cousin of Jeroni Basté Wittig of celler de l'Abadia a Gratallops and his wife's family has also been making wine for a while in the DO Ribeira Sacra of Galicia. After years of collaborating with both wineries, in 2007 he decided to start making his own wine according to his personal taste. The name Peites in all his wines refers to the little village in Galicia where his in-laws come from and is a tribute to them for encouraging him in his own venture.

At the moment Josep Alfons is making three different wines with the technical assistance of his enolog cousin Jeroni, the Peites jove, Peites criança and Clos Peites, the last of which is barrel-aged for 30 months. Although Mas Basté and celler de l'Abadia both share the same vineyards and facilities, they have a different winemaking philosophies and styles and thus their wines have a different character. Currently Mas Basté produces about 20,000 bottles a year.

J. Alfons Cazurra Basté
owner

GPS
41.192746
0.777899

Mas Basté
Gratallops, *Carrer de l'Era, 5*

Visits: Not currently open for public visits
Contact: 622060136 | info@cellermasbaste.com
Website: www.cellermasbaste.com

Peites 2011 has a lightly earthy nose to it that gives way to a body of light spice and is relatively easy on the palate. Fruity and plush in the body, it leads in to a dry, lingering finish.
Grenache, Syrah

● | 14% | 10€ |

Peites Criança 2009 starts out with a light hit of dark fruits and minerality to the aromas that then shift in to a slightly earthy quality. The body is quite light and balanced overall with a good dose of acids and the smallest hit of oak elements. The spices and acids linger in to the finish.
80% Carignan, 20% Syrah, 10% Cab Sauvignon

● | 14,5% | 20€ |

Jordi Torrella
manager & enolog

GPS
41.229504
0.866809

Mas d'en Blei
La Morera de Montsant, *Mas d'en Blei*

Visits: Available every day calling ahead, they can welcome 2-12 people. The visit to the vineyards, cellar and a tasting of their wines costs 6€ a person.
Contact: 686246679,977262031 | info@masdenblei.com
Website: www.masdenblei.com
Languages: English, French, Portuguese

Despite being not much more than a stone's throw outside of Poboleda, Mas d'en Blei is technically in the La Morera municipality. But whatever the village it's attached to, this old stone masia with 17.5 hectares of land surrounding it dates back from 1756 and sits beautifully by the side of a stream that feeds in to the Siurana River.

With oak trees dotted about the hills of the property and the remnants of old stone terraces popping up here and there, they started clearing the land from 2004-2005. In 2006 they planted their first vines and in 2010, finished construction on the new cellar that sits opposite the old house on the other side of the stream.

Their Mas d'en Blei white, Clos Martina was released in 2010 with an initial production of 3,255 bottles. The red, Blei they've released in 2013 with 9,200 bottles. Little by little they're increasing production with enolog, Jordi Torrella guiding its path. Torrella, who has worked in a number of wineries in the area, is also managing Celler de l'Era, a new winery in the DO Montsant in nearby Cornudella del Montsant. As the Mas d'en Blei winery grows further in this bucolic little valley, they also plan to release a Mistela and a Vi Ranci of Muscat, which are traditional grape based drinks made in the region.

Clos Martina 2010 initially presents a woody nose with a dose of roasted chestnut. The body is strong and more of a New World style upon first opening. The finish is quick with few acids present. As it breathes, more minerality comes up. It's a very different style Priorat white, but one that manages to be very articulate at the same time.

84% White Grenache, 10% Pedro Ximénez, 6% Xarel·lo

 | 13.5% | 12-14€

Negre 2010 has a rich nose with aromas of dark cherry, currant, spices, and a tiny dose of black pepper. It's large and filling in the mouth with a plush texture that starts out with a fresh character initially. The minerality is downplayed overall and held at bay with balanced tannins and acids. The finish lingers quite well, is fully enjoyable and shows a very well crafted wine from their rather young vines.

Grenache, Carignan, Syrah

 | 13.5% | 15€

Vineyards with the Montsant bluff

Valentí Llagostera
owner

GPS
41.235565
0.84692

Mas Doix
Poboleda, *Carrer de Carme, 115*

Visits: They have a number of options starting with a basic tasting for two people at 15€ per person. They also have a two hour visit to the cellar and tasting that starts at 25€ per person for two people. Then they have a guided tasting, full visit, and lunch that starts at 100€ per person for two people. Each of these options decreases in price for larger groups. Call ahead for exact prices and reservations.
Contact: 628800466 | visit@masdoix.com
Website: www.masdoix.com
Languages: English, French, Italian

After years of feeding grapes from their old vineyards in to the Poboleda cooperative, in 1998 Ramon and Valentí Llagostera decided along with their cousin Josep Maria Doix that it was time to start making their own wines again. They are the proud owners of beautiful Carignan and Grenache vineyards on steep slopes that were replanted in 1902 shortly after the devastation of phylloxera.

So, since 1999 Mas Doix has been crafting wines that have become some of the best in Priorat, slowly growing while sticking to their desire to almost exclusively grow native grapes to the area, namely Grenache and Carignan. These days they make about 50,000 bottles a year from their 18 hectares of vineyards ranging from 20-110 years-old and planted on slopes at 350-600 meters of altitude. As of 2012 their enolog is Sandra Doix, daughter of Josep Maria Doix.

Anyone who visits Poboleda can stop in to their cellar right on the main road through town with its modern interior and patio in the front. For those with enough time, it's a real treat to go and see their oldest vineyards tucked back in the mountains on the other side of town with gorgeous views of northern Priorat, Poboleda and the Montsant mountains. There the vines tenaciously cling to the crumbling slate soil that makes up the slopes. They can even organize a traditional lunch alongside the winery visit.

Bottle archive

Les Crestes 2010 is from their vines that are 20-25 years old. There's a great wealth of fresh fruits in the nose that really show the grapes well. It's refreshing on the palate and cleans out the mouth well during a meal. Great for many dishes, it's also a pleasant wine to have on its own as well with its quick finish and good acidity lingering just enough to be pleasant.

80% Grenache, 10% Carignan, 10% Syrah

 ● | 15% | 14€ | ⚖

Salanques 2006 is a blend of their 60-80 year-old vines. It has multi-layered aromas to the nose with touches of herbs and minerality. Light and gentle overall, but it picks up spice in the body with red fruits and other aspects of brightness. There's good acidity that's overall well-balanced with the body.

65% Grenache, 20% Carignan, 10% Syrah, 3% Cab Sauvignon, 2% Merlot

 ● | 15% | 24€

Doix 2008 is a blend of grapes from their 110 year-old Carignan and 85 year-old Grenache grown on steep slopes, aged for 16 months in new French oak barrels. It has a warmer nose with a good deal more chocolate to it. The body carries this to some degree, but at the same time, it still allows for a good deal of acidity to come through as well as the rich, red fruits. So, despite the depth of the wine, it would still pair well with many meals.

55% Grenache, 45% Carignan

 ● | 14,5% | 75€ | ✹

MAS DOIX

Josep Garriga Anguera
owner

GPS
41.170417
0.744087

Mas Garrian
El Molar, *Camí de les Rieres, Mas Camperol*

Visits: From 2-20 people can visit at a cost of 10€ per person including a tasting of their wines, although the fee is waived with a bottle purchase. Call for availability and reservations.
Contact: 977262118,639623269 | masgarrian@gmail.com
Languages: English, French

On the right side of the rambling river road that passes between El Lloar and El Molar sits the property of Mas Camperol. Built during the mining boom in 1870 by a wine merchant who made his money in the Americas, it's a rather fascinating house. It's unlike any other in the area with construction techniques make it look like it could withstand a nuclear blast. Josep Garriga Anguera's grandfather bought the property in 1948 and it was about 30 years ago that they started planting new vineyards on the property and selling the grapes to local collectives.

Around 13 years ago, they planted more vineyards amongst the olive groves, bringing the total to seven hectares and starting the winery of Mas Garrian (a portmanteau of the first syllable of Josep's two last names). Their first vintage was in 1999 and since then, they've grown to producing about 12,000 bottles a year.

The cellar is in the bottom of the home and while compact, provides them with all the space they need to make their wines. The top of the cellar has made for a very nice balcony at the back of the house from which they have a wonderful view of the Siurana River as it passes by, just before leaving Priorat.

In the cellar

Clos Severí Junior 2009 has a nose that starts out rather tight with red fruits that carry in to a spicy and jammy body with a good degree of prune elements to it. It has a soft texture on the palate that leads in to a quick finish. It's not immensely complex overall, but is enjoyable and very approachable.
Grenache, Carignan, Merlot

● | 13,5% | 9€

Clos Severí 2006 has a fat, plump nose with wild blackberry running through it. The slippery texture to the wine shows off clay like qualities in the body along with strong tannins and acids. As it opens, more herbal notes start to appear as well as a vanilla underpinning to the nose.
65% Grenache, 25% Carignan, 10% Syrah

● | 14,5% | 15€

Clos del Sarraí 2008 opens with a large, warm nose laced with mineral and tobacco aromas. It's dry overall, but with a good, balanced acidity. Tar red plum comes up in the body and with air, a tar element becomes more pronounced.
50% Grenache, 40% Carignan, 10% Syrah

● | 14,5% | 15€

Mas del Camperol 2004 has a rich, big nose of dark fruits and great herbal components. This comes in to the body and the herbal components grow as well as the minerality. The oak comes up a touch as it gets air, but still stays at bay and gets out of the way completely when it pulls out in to the finish that leaves the herbal notes lingering as well as a hit of spiciness.
Grenache, Carignan, Syrah, Cab Sauvignon

● | 15% | 25€

Pere Rovira
owner

GPS
41.154101
0.765308

Mas d'en Gil
Bellmunt del Priorat *Carretera Falset-Bellmunt, km 4.5*

Visits: Not currently open for public visits
Contact: 977830192 | mail@masdengil.com
Website: www.masdengil.com

Coming from Falset to Bellmunt makes for a much different landscape that what is seen further north in Priorat. Here, the rolling hills sport fewer terraces and vines carpet them in great abundance. On the left side of the road, just before Bellmunt is one of the heaviest concentrations of vines and this is where Mas d'en Gil calls home.

A unique property and a landmark in Priorat wine history, Mas d'en Gil seems to have been built originally in the late 1700s. It was owned for many years by Francesc Gil from Reus, but was purchased by the Barril family in 1931 who produced there some of the first bottled wines in Priorat. During that time it was known as Masia Barril, and their wines were known beyond Spain's borders. In 1998 Pere Rovira, a winemaker with a long history and experience in Penedès, fell in love with the place and decided to purchase it to start making wine in Priorat. In 2000 he bought the neighboring property bringing Mas d'en Gil to a total of 125 hectares. The estate is idyllic, surrounded by the view of the Llaberia and Montsant mountains and with terraced vineyards that look like gardens, it receives a great deal of the "garbinada", a wind that blows southwest from the sea and provides a fresher micro-climate. They have maintained the diversity of crops in the estate which has helped them to farm organically as well as biodynamically in an effort to work in harmony with the environment.

From the 45ha of vineyards they now grow, they bring all the grapes to their cellar in the masia and work with all the 43 little parcels separately before final blending. Pere has a devoted passion to making honest wines from the land that show the locale as clearly as possible and somehow he manages to continue doing this despite making 80,000 bottles a year now. Of course, he holds back a few cards every now and again as seen with the bottling of their Gran Buig which is only in very select years that, to date have only been 1998 and 2007. These days Pere has passed the managing duties of the winery to his younger daughter, Marta.

As they're a large farm with many different crops grown, in addition to the wines, they produce olive oil from their 12ha of trees as well as high quality vinegar (they're the only vinegar producers in Priorat). It would be great to say that all of this is available in the nice shop they have onsite after a visit to the impressive and well maintained masia, but despite looking like they could receive guests tomorrow, they aren't open to the public and keep focusing on making their high quality wines.

Coma Alta 2010 has a nose that heaves deeply with minerality, but there is a surprisingly degree of earthiness to it despite being a white wine. Incredibly light and easy across the palate, but still with a strong foundation that's not to be ignored. Clean in the finish, it leaves an interesting salty note as it departs.
85% White Grenache, 15% Viognier

 | 15% | 24-28€

Coma Vella 2007 opens with a complex nose of gentle minerality, light red fruit aromas, and a touch of licorice to the bottom of it. Initially fresh in the mouth with raspberry notes, it opens up its acidity and light tannins quite quickly to wash over the palate. The finish pulls out nicely, departing quickly with just the smallest touch of lingering acidity and spices to make for a very approachable meal wine with solid character.
60% Grenache, 30% Carignan, 10% Syrah

 | 15% | 24-28€

Clos Fontà 2007 opens with a nose of dark fruits and earthy notes. Across the body, it's luscious and swims in deep aromas and rich spices like white pepper that sit atop a meaty, delicious foundation. Despite the large depth to the body, the finish is light and easy, leaving just a touch of all the best elements of the wine as it departs. As it breathes, the minerality comes up more.
60% Carignan, 40% Grenache

 | 15% | 45-50€ | ✹

Mireia Pujol-Busquets
manager & enolog

GPS
41.205087
0.778462

Mas Igneus

Gratallops, *Carretera Gratallops-La Vilella Baixa, km 1.8*

Visits: Call ahead for availability and pricing based on group size and activities desired.
Contact: 977262259,676293435 | celler@masigneus.com
Website: www.masigneus.com
Languages: English

On the top of a mountain near Gratallops, at Coll de la Vaca (Cow's Pass) there sits the still-inhabited 13th century hermitage of Mare de Déu de la Consolació (Our Lady of Consolation) keeping watch over all below. Along the road up to this small building lie great swaths of terraced vineyards that belong to Mas Igneus' Costers de l'Ermita estate and which they'll happily show to those who visit in order to take in the stunning views out over the whole Priorat.

Once introduced to these Grenache and Carignan vines, you come back down to the bend in the road between the Trossos del Priorat and Buil & Giné wineries to enter the modern building designed by Alfons Soldevila that houses Mas Igneus. Some locals in the area know it less by name than by appearance and call it "the bus station" as it indeed has some resemblance with its long form and metal framing. But, inside they produce about 50,000 bottles a year from their 10 hectares of organic vineyards that spread around the cellar like a terraced bowl.

Although this winery was finished only in 2004, Mas Igneus was founded some years earlier in 1996 by winemakers Josep Maria Albet i Noya, Josep Maria Pujol-Busquets and initially the Poboleda Cooperative. In 2004, the two friends and the cooperative parted ways which in turn led to their starting the Mas Igneus winery. Albet i Noya's fam-

Barrels aging

ily has been growing vines in the Penedès region for over a hundred years and he was one of the first winemakers to produce organic wines there back in the late 1970s. On the other hand, Pujol-Busquets and his wife have a winery in the Alella region just north of Barcelona and their daughter Mireia recently became the manager of Mas Igneus while also working in the family winery in Alella.

Barranc Blanc 2011 is aged in acacia and chestnut barrels for about three months. The nose is rich and full of pear aromas with a hint of guava and other tropical elements. The body has generally sweet elements, but also carries in the aromas from the nose to form a pleasant, balanced white with a great deal of unique qualities and enough acidic elements in the finish to allow for good meal pairings but at the same time having a strong enough body to drink alone.

90% White Grenache, 10% Pedro Ximénez

 | 14.5% | 11€ |

Barranc Negre 2010 spends three months in oak to give off a light, gentle nose with slight hints of red fruits at the bottom of it and dusty aspects. The body has a surprising degree of acidity to it and red fruit elements dominate. It has a light finish with hints of fresh mint which then falls a bit short.

75% Grenache, 25% Carignan

 | 15% | 11€ |

FA 206 2010 has a nose that's large blackberry with hints of licorice. It develops and opens a great deal with just a touch of air to give floral and other elements from the locale. The body is light, balanced and sits well on the palate. Some of the aromas from the nose transfer in to the body, but it presents more of a mineral front and the finish lingers more with soft acids.

75% Grenache, 20% Carignan, 5% Cab Sauvignon

 | 15% | 18€

MAS IGNEUS

Sara Pérez
owner & enolog

GPS
41.174915
0.791868

Mas Martinet
Gratallops, *Carretera Falset-Gratallops, km 6*

Visits: Not currently open for public visits
Contact: 629238236 | masmartinet@masmartinet.com
Website: www.masmartinet.com

One of the "Big Five" wineries of Priorat, Mas Martinet is secluded and tucked down off the road from Falset to Gratallops. As the story goes, biology professor Josep Lluís Pérez arrived in Priorat with his family in 1981 to direct the recently created enology school in Falset. During those first few years he and his students recuperated old vineyards and experimented with different local grapes. In 1986 he purchased his first vineyards and in 1989 he participated in the group project of René Barbier and the others.

Mas Martinet's wines gained a great deal of fame and they started using more of the native Grenache and Carignan grapes. In 2000, Josep Lluís' daughter, Sara planted the highest vineyard in Priorat with llicorella soil called, Escurçons ("vipers" in English) that sits at 600m with a glorious view and is one part of their current 12 hectares of vineyards. Also in 2000, Josep Lluís officially passed the mantle of Mas Martinet to his daughter to focus his efforts on a more experimental consulting company he started in Porrera, Mas Martinet Assessoraments.

In the last 13 years, Sara Pérez has continued to produce stellar wines as well as push the boundaries of Mas Martinet. Moreover, she is not only one of the top women winemakers in Spain but she is also making a separate line of extremely interesting wines called, Bellvisos together with her husband René Barbier IV of the other Priorat titan, Clos Mogador. As if all of this wasn't enough, this hyperactive couple also have another winery in neighboring DO Montsant under the name Venus "La Universal" and another one in Ribeira Sacra, Galicia.

An example of Mas Martinet's continued innovation is their producing a large amount of their wines via unlined concrete tanks as well as aging in amphorae since 2011. They started using the amphorae when they were able to find a provider just down the Ebre River from Priorat in Miravet. They are currently farming organically and only use wild yeasts from their vineyards.

Martinet Bru 2008 has very pleasant mineral notes in the nose along with an underlying touch of chocolate and wild herbs. Approachable for general drinkers, the body carries the minerality as well as herbs and adds touches of dried fig and prune. These elements linger pleasantly in the finish.
Grenache, Carignan, Cab Sauvignon, Merlot, Syrah

● | 14,5% | 18€ | ⚖

Els Escurçons 2009 has delicate aromas from the Grenache with small traces of fennel. The body is wonderfully bright and introduces small licorice flavors. Soft across the palate, it dances down in to the finish in this very balanced fashion that carries out to the last touch of mature plums and almonds.
100% Grenache

● | 15% | 48-50€ | ✻

Clos Martinet 2007 has a nose like the earth just before the rain hits. The body has a most interesting character, initially showing a good deal of strength, but then backing off immediately to let out the spices and herbs of the vineyard from where it grows. Herbal notes come up in the finish and fade out with lingering hints of fennel and anis.
Grenache, Carignan, Syrah, Cab Sauvignon, Merlot

● | 14,5% | 48-50€

Camí de Pesseroles 2009 shows a forceful nose of dark fruits although still buttery. While large in the body, the mineral character comes through well. Larger tannins appear while the acids are taken down a notch, but still linger in to the finish. Despite the overall size of the wine, the small, lurking astringency to it would still work well for select food pairings like aged cheeses.
60% Carignan, 40% Grenache

● | 15% | 55€ | ✻

Jordi Masdéu
owner & enolog

GPS
41.233687
0.845153

Mas la Mola
Poboleda, *Carrer Raval, 4*

Visits: Not currently open for public visits
Contact: 651034221 | info@maslamola.com
Website: www.maslamola.com

Jordi Masdéu and Alessandro Marchesan are two wine enthusiasts who were roommates in London while working in different wine sales capacities. In 2007 they decided to make their own style of Priorat wines and in this, it appears that they've largely succeeded. Producing about 12-15,000 bottles a year from their small cellar in the center of Poboleda, they export some 95% of their wines and in total, 70% if them end up in restaurants.

But, they're not ones to turn their backs on tradition. After all, the vines that they're making use of have been in the possession of the Ferrando family for 150 years. Also, they aren't afraid to try using supposedly non-commercial grapes such as Hairy Grenache which, when mixed with the more well known grapes of Priorat makes for bottles that have a very unique taste. Because in the end, they're young winemakers and they want to invest in their cellar to make wines that stand out.

It is worth noting that Jordi also has a small winery in the DO Conca de Barberà with another friend called, Molí dels Capellans.

Winery exterior

Blanc 2010 is an unusual blend which is the opposite of most whites in the region. It has a mineral nose with touches of citrus and minerality defining it. Fresh and bright across the palate, it embraces the mouth with a refreshing fullness. The finish kicks up a touch of acidity to linger through in to the end, opening up the mouth.

70% Macabeu, 30% White Grenache

 | 13,5% | 22-24€

L'Expressió del Priorat 2011 is immediately potent in the nose with dark fruits and a touch of cedar. The body is similar with sweeter, bolder fruits than other wines in the region. It's round and a touch buttery on the palate and would be immediately approachable by most anyone and offers up and interesting take on the young wine.

40% Grenache, 40% Carignan, 10% Syrah, 10% Cab Sauvignon

 | 14% | 12€

Mas la Mola Negre 2007 opens with a mineral nose that has a healthy red cherry aspect to it. While light across the palate, in the body the cherry aspects of the nose shift to general red fruit elements with a hint of strawberry. A bit chewy in texture, the wine finishes quickly with a burst of acidity.

Grenache, Carignan, Cab Sauvignon, Syrah

 | 14,5% | 22-24€ | ✹

Mas la Mola La Vinyeta Vella 2007 starts out rather closed with a touch of minerality, lime, and licorice in the nose. As it opens, the body presents a dry texture and a good dose of acidity, plum, and lemon peel. As it breathes, white pepper notes come up, and the body gets spicy and a little wilder. The pepper notes continue in to the finish with a lingering acidity. With even more time to breathe, burnt caramel and chocolate notes appear.

Grenache, Carignan

 | 15% | 35€ | ✹

GPS
41.233478
0.872306

Mas Perinet
La Morera, *Mas Perinet*

Visits: Available in the mornings on weekends, they welcome groups of 4-20 people to visit and taste the wines at a cost of 10€ per person.
Contact: 977827113 | visit@masperinet.com
Website: www.masperinet.com
Languages: English, French

Sitting just east of Poboleda, this winery has been something of an enigma to the winemakers in the village. Large, modern, and striking, they lay claim to a quite significant 23 hectares of vineyards that surround the cellar and roll up and down the terraced hills. They stopped producing wine for two years though which gave the winery an appearance of being completely closed. As gossip is a standard form of currency in villages, the questions ran around as to whether the winery had been abandoned or sold or something else. In the end, Mas Perinet has returned to production with their 2012 harvest.

It's good to see the winery come back to a life that began in 1998 when the three current owners bought this historic estate of 300 hectares that was fully covered in vineyards prior to the arrival of Phylloxera in 1894. In 1999 they began planting vines again and building the cellar, finishing in 2004 with their first estate vintage. Their first official vintage was actually in 2002, but it was made with grapes purchased from other vineyards. Of the 33ha of planted vineyards, 23 are in the DOQ Priorat while the rest lie within DO Montsant where they make the wines Gotia and Clos Maria in a smaller cellar. Their enolog for all wines is Josep Serra.

The cellar is a gravity fed system and nothing short of impressive. Heavily modern and angular from the outside, it's set in to the hill. Inside, they have a production facility that can produce up to 160,000 bottles a year. But, it's the barrel cellar below this that's even more impressive as it was built in this organic, Gaudí-esque style with support columns that look like tree trunks or deep roots depending on how many local wines you've tasted that day.

Perinet 2006 has a nose with light minerality and delicate aromas of red fruit and earthy minerality. The red fruit becomes more pronounced in the body and is quite well balanced with a nice, bright acidity to make for a very pleasing wine overall. The finish carries this out in a juicy finish. While somewhat typical in general, it presents a slightly different style of wine for the region.
35% Carignan, 19% Syrah, 16% Grenache, 15% Cab Sauvignon, 14% Merlot

 | 14,5% | 15-17€

Perinet + Plus 2005 is only made in select years. The nose is soft, delicate and dusty with the old Carignan aspects and dark fruits emerging as it decants. Much of this carries in to the body and forms a very well balanced and nicely structured wine that in the finish disperses very quickly leaving just a small touch of the dustiness on the palate.
56% Carignan, 31% Grenache, 13% Syrah

 | 15% | 50€

Main production tanks

Tucked away on a steep road on the side of La Vilella Alta, the Mas Perla winery sits on top of a hill in what used to be a farming warehouse that they refurbished in 2007. Before that, though, they were already making wines in a rented space since 2005.

The owners are a diverse group of people with a common interest in wine, comprising Bordeaux wine merchant Philippe Bourlon, superstar enolog Gilles Pauquet of Cheval Blanc and Yquem fame (both $500 a bottle), and former banker Amadeu Alerany whose family owned vineyards in Priorat. Before 2005 Amadeu, who is originally from Gratallops and was born in the house that is now hotel Cal Llop, was selling his grapes to the local collective. But, after finding the right partners interested in making high quality wines in Priorat, he decided to start his own winery.

In total they harvest from about 10ha of vineyards, one of which dates back to 1927. Although they made some wine in 2005, their first official vintage was in 2006. They currently produce between 20-30,000 bottles a year depending on the harvest, and they export most of them. Their wines are quite fantastic and can easily stay 20 years in the bottle.

Amadeu Alerany
owner

GPS
41.22436
0.780318

Mas Perla
La Vilella Alta, *Carrer les Eres*

Visits: They are offered on a very limited basis to small groups. Call for reservations and details.
Contact: 646748500 | a.alerany@telefonica.net
Website: www.masperla.cat

Imaginacio 2006 doesn't see any time in the oak. It allows the fruit to come through a great deal more in the nose and the body and is a very smooth, easy to drink wine that's enjoyable. It still has a good boost of tannins and balanced acidity, but the wine doesn't overpower itself. Sadly, they don't produce any new vintages of the wine.
Grenache

🔴 | 14,5% | 15€ |

Mas Perla 2007 has a relatively soft nose given the time spent in the oak. While there is a touch of American oak its characteristics were much less pronounced and it made for a much rounder wine overall. The body is soft on the palate allowing deeper spices to come up compared to previous vintages.
Grenache

🔴 | 14,5% | 20€

Salvador Burgos
owner

GPS
41.225128
0.845751

Mas Sinén
Poboleda, *Mas Sinén*

Visits: Reservations are required especially if requesting it in English. Tours include a walk over the steep terraces, a visit to the cellar, and a tasting afterwards of their three main organic wines for 10€.
Contact: 696094509,619328534 | burgosporta@massinen.com
Website: www.massinen.com

Upon arriving in the charming 12th century village of Poboleda, the exact direction you need to go in order to get to Mas Sinén isn't immediately obvious. A quick drop down Carrer Major though will bring you to the first of many signs that guide you through the village and out the other side, winding your way through the hills and many terraced vineyards of others who make their wine in Poboleda.

As the road continues, it's easy to think that perhaps upon arrival, a wild boar in the area will show up to valet park your car at the winery. But, long before you reach Porrera (as this was the old donkey road that used to connect the two villages), the bowl of slate terraces that wrap around the stone winery of Mas Sinén opens before you. Here Salvador Burgos and Conxita Porta have been making wine for a decade and warmly welcome visitors wandering by. Salvador, who was the president of the Poboleda cooperative for many years, has been growing vines for about 30 years. These days Mas Sinén has 14 hectares of organic vineyards ranging from 300 to 500m of altitude, distributed between this little valley and another nearby mountain slope.

While the winery building is a lovely stone structure, it's actually quite modern given that the 300 year-old masia that was on the property was nearly abandoned when they started the winery in 2003. That first vintage, which they produced in another winery, was of only 2,000 bottles.

Sloped and terraced vineyards

Since then they've been slowly growing to the 20,000 bottles of annual production they have now, although their goal is to reach a maximum of 25,000. The wines certainly reflect the couple's character, but they also consult with Priorat enology superhero, Toni Coca.

Salvador and Conxita love to promote Priorat's wine culture and to show visitors the gorgeous views of the surrounding mountains, give them a taste of water from the ancient fountain set on top of the vineyards (quite a rare thing in the dry soils of Priorat), eat figs from their trees when they're in season, and even let them enjoy a picnic in the area they have for that.

Blanc Mas Sinén 2010 is White Grenache that loves to show it in the nose with the advanced minerality and citric aromas. The body is light and delicate across the palate with a slight petrol aspect that shows off the acids and well built aspects of the grape. The finish is bright and fresh.

100% White Grenache

 | 15% | 16-17€

Petit Mas Sinén 2009 spends six months in the barrels and has a color that simply glows in the glass. The nose has spice, leather, and great slate elements. While large with red fruits, you can really taste the grapes and the locale in the body.

Grenache, Carignan, Cab Sauvignon, Syrah, Merlot

 | 14,5% | 11-13€ | ⚖ | ✹

Negre Mas Sinén 2008 is a blend that receives 12 months of barrel aging. It has a wonderful spicy, herbaceous nose that's rich in minerals with an underlying licorice aspect. The body is potent with leather elements and a touch of vanilla from the barrels. While strong, it's quite well balanced with tannins coming up a bit in the finish.

Grenache, Carignan, Cab Sauvignon, Syrah

 | 15% | 22-25€

Ricard Mayol
owner

GPS
41.212605
0.810268

Mayol
Torroja del Priorat, *Carrer de La Bassa, 24*

Visits: Available every day except Monday for 2-18 people, the price per person ranges from 8-12€ depending activities desired. Call for reservations.
Contact: 977839395 | ccllcr@mayol.eu
Website: www.mayol.eu

It's not hard to find Mayol as their small shop with a tasting room and offices above it, is located in Torroja beneath some large shade trees and the large, "Welcome to Torroja" sign that is oddly enough not visible from the main road. Their actual winery is a bit further away, though, on the road from Torroja to Escaladei.

Ricard Mayol's family has had a long history in Priorat, they estimate it goes back some 500 years and for at least the last five generations, they've been based in Torroja. As he likes to say, they didn't "fall in love with Priorat" but were always here. Having this base helped a great deal in planting some of their first vines some 40 years ago, although they own others that are nearly 70 years old. In 2000, they formed the company and in 2004 they made their first wines in a rented space. In 2007 they built the cellar which they're now looking to expand.

In total, they currently produce about 40,000 bottles a year with the help of consultant enolog Toni Coca, and export some 86% of it internationally. And, as of 2013, they are a fully certified organic winery.

Vineyards

Roser 2011 is a blend that sees five months aging in oak barrels. It's a rather small production of 3,500 bottles a year. The nose has the light, summery fruits of Macabeu but an underpinning of minerality from the White Grenache. It's bright in the mouth with fuzziness at the bottom and something of a hardness to it that comes from the aging regimen. The finish is overall bright quick.

90% Macabeu, 10% White Grenache

 | 14,5% | 14€

Glop 2010 sees four months of barrel aging. It's quite stony in the nose with a small touch of dark fruit to it, but mostly it boasts the minerality. This transfers in to the body with a dose of acidity to make it well suited for having with meals. The body lets up a bit short of the finish which clears out quickly, leaving just a bit of fruit in the mouth to chew on. It is typical of the younger vineyards in the region, but it with character.

60% Grenache, 20% Syrah, 20% Carignan

 | 14,5% | 11€

Torroja des de dins 2009 sees eight months of oak aging. The nose is like warm raisin bread but this blows off in the glass to reveal slight dark fruits and minerality which are both quite mellow overall. It's quite light on the palate and generally easy to drink with a kick of acidity, red fruits, and a tiny chocolate aspect at the end which linger in to the finish.

Grenache, Carignan, Syrah, Cab Sauvignon

 | 14,5% | 16€ |

Brogit 2010 sees eight months of oak aging. The nose is like warm raisin bread but this blows off in the glass to reveal slight dark fruits and minerality which are both quite mellow overall. It's quite light on the palate and generally easy to drink with a kick of acidity, red fruits, and a tiny chocolate aspect at the end which linger in to the finish.

Grenache, Carignan, Syrah

 | 15% | 23€

MAYOL

Javier López and Víctor Gallegos met while studying enology at UC Davis some 30 years ago and during that time they visited Priorat which left a strong impression. In 2000 they acquired 20 hectares of land that included 1.5ha of 100 year-old vines between Torroja and Porrera, and in 2004 they rented some more vineyards to produce their first vintage. They now make upwards of 40,000 bottles a year, focusing on the new/old fresher style of Priorat. This philosophy is a direct reflection of Victor's work as head winemaker of SeaSmoke Cellars in Santa Barbara County, California. There he makes unique Pinot Noir wines that have a cult following (one of which even appeared in the movie "Sideways"). In addition to Victor, the Melis enology team also includes consultants Claude Gross of Chateau de la Négly in Languedoc and Toni Sánchez of Solà d'Ares.

Obrador 2009 opens up full in the nose with bright minerality and fresh, red fruits. These elements come in to the body as well and present an alive and exciting bottle.
54% Grenache, 24% Syrah, 12% Carignan, 10% Cab Sauv

● | 14,5% | 12€ | ⚖ | ✻

Javier López Botella
owner

Melis
Torroja del Priorat, *Balandra, 54*

Visits: Not currently open for public visits
Contact: 937313021 | info@melispriorat.com
Website: www.melispriorat.com

Elix 2007 initially puts out red fruits with an underlying smoothness to the nose, as well as a touch of white pepper. Smooth and plush on the palate, it shows a dusty plum aspect as it decants. With a clean fresh finish, it's an overall very classy and elegant wine.
Grenache, Cab Sauvignon, Carignan, Syrah
🔴 | 15% | 30€

Melis 2006 shows great aromas from the start with fresh red fruits, white pepper and a poignant minerality. It's dusty and smooth in the body with hints of chocolate and tobacco coming out with time. Big, bright, and spicy overall, it consistently maintains elegance and refinement.
62% Grenache, 19% Carignan, 13% Cab Sauv, 6% Syrah
🔴 | 15,5% | 65€ | ✦

Meritxell Pallejà admits to not having been the best of students in high school, but when she encountered the enology program in Falset that her brother was attending, she says that she immediately took to it and even pursued two more degrees at the Tarragona University. Once finished with her studies she worked at several wineries abroad and in the Priorat comarca including the cooperative in Capçanes, Fra Fulcó, and the now legendary, Álvaro Palacios in Gratallops.

While her brother has a small vineyard near Falset and she has two in Gratallops, she currently makes her Nita wine in the facilites of Vinícola del Priorat with select grapes purchased from various wineries. She hopes to start making wine with her own grapes in the near future. Her first vintage of Nita was in 2004 which totaled 15,000 bottles but these days she's producing around 32,000 bottles a year. While she continues her enology work for other cellars, the Nita brand has proven to be quite successful in no small part due to a lack of oak aging, general freshness, and wonderful approachability to the wine year after year.

Meritxell Pallejà
owner & enolog

Meritxell Pallejà
Gratallops, *Masets, 11*

Visits: Not currently open for public visits
Contact: 670960735 | info@nita.cat
Website: www.nita.cat

Nita 2010 is named after Meritxell's grandmother Juanita whose house was called Cal Nita. The nose opens with violet qualities and touches of minerality. The body expands on this a great deal with downplayed red fruit aromas downplayed as well as mineral elements hanging in the background. It is a very even handed bottle that sets itself up very well as an extremely pleasant wine to drink for most any company and situation.

Grenache, Carignan, Cab Sauvignon, Syrah

● | 14,5% | 11 12€ | ⚖

Judit Llop
manager & enolog

GPS
41.150264
0.742907

Morlanda
Bellmunt del Priorat, *Mas Subirà*

Visits: It's free to visit, but availability is limited. Call to make a reservation beforehand, weekdays are preferred.
Contact: 977831309 | morlanda@morlanda.com
Website: www.morlanda.com
Languages: English

While one of the most southern wineries in DOQ Priorat, the easiest way to visit Morlanda is by arriving from DO Montsant. There, when coming from Falset, just before El Masroig, a dirt road with a sign for "l'Ermita de les Pinyeres" points in the initial direction of the winery. This hermitage is an interesting historical stop for any visitor with some extra time, but following the winding road past farmhouses and over a small dry creek, one eventually comes upon the very vast 82 hectares estate of the winery. Of these, only 9ha have been planted with vineyards, with an additional 4ha of vineyards located elsewhere near Bellmunt.

Taking its name from the highest mountain surrounding the property, this winery was created in 1997 by four friends who shared their love of wine, including a former minister of agriculture, two Falset natives, and the CEO of the Penedès wine giant Freixenet (in a personal capacity). The same year they founded the winery, they built the modern cellar that sits in the middle of the vineyards. In 2001, it formally became part of the Freixenet group who owns about 20 wineries nationally. Locally, enolog Judit Llop manages all the day-to-day business as well as hosting visits depending on availability.

The winery now produces about 46,000 bottles a year, which may seem like a large production, but it's just 1/3 the production of their other winery in neighboring DO Montsant that they built in 2001.

Blanc 2011 starts out with a floral nose of honeysuckle and apricot with just a touch of minerality lurking in the shadows. In the body, tones of lemon peel come forward as well as a general aspect of tartness. It stays quite strong across the palate and all the way in to the finish. The White Grenache makes for a big wine that doesn't show much integration with the Macabeu as others.
85% White Grenache, 15% Macabeu

 | 14% | €

Mas de Subirà 2009 has a slight, smoky nose. Good acids form in the body and speak to the clay soils from where it's grown. A slight roasted corn aspect comes up as it breathes and the wine is overall mild and agreeable.
60% Grenache, 30% Carignan, 10% Cab Sauvignon

● | 15% | 14€

Vi de Guarda Negre 2007 has a warm, earthy nose with a touch of tobacco. The body is slightly mineral with more red fruits taking over and a general dryness with larger acids. It would pair well with meals despite the lengthy aging.
50% Grenache, 50% Carignan

 | 15% | 22€

Prior Terrae 2009 has a slightly granitic, red fruit nose with even brighter fruits in the body that shift in to cherry flavors. The tannins work up a bit as it breathes and carry in to the finish. With more decanting, a chocolate quality comes in to play in the body.
Grenache, Carignan

 | 15% | €

The Priorat vineyards of Noguerals are located up in the Barranc de la Bruixa or, Witch's Gorge area, in Mas de l'Abella. While they also have a winery in DO Montsant in neighboring Cornudella, they started up their Priorat enterprise in 1999 in the section of the masia that used to be an old barn that they had to rehabilitate as it was nearly abandoned. The masia itself is a lovely old stone building, but is in a crumbling state as it was split via inheritance and hasn't been touched. Despite the state of partial renovations, it's still a scenic setting of old oaks and small hills that look out upon the steep llicorella mountains surrounding the estate.

Across the bumpy dirt road that comes in to this area from Cornudella sit their vineyards which they planted in 2000. They produced their first vintages in 2002 from grapes that they bought from other vineyards but these days they use their own grapes from 3.5 hectares. They produce 8,000 bottles a year in their small cellar in Mas de l'Abella that was finished in 2007.

Ramon Alzamora
owner

GPS
41.24814
0.878347

Nogguerals
La Morera de Montsant, *Barranc de la Bruixa*

Visits: They conduct visits at their other winery in Cornudella on weekends with a maximum of 10 people. The price is 15€ per person although it's waived with purchase.
Contact: 650033546 | noguerals@hotmail.com
Website: www.noguerals.com
Languages: English, French

Abellars 2007 spends 12 months in a 50/50 mix of new and old oak. It has dark fruit mixed with a touch of spice and minerality. It fills in softly on the palate with the spice still coming up as well as a little black pepper and anis. The finish is neutral and clean.
50% Grenache, 25% Carignan, 15% Cab Sauv 10% Syrah

 | 14,5% | 18-20€

Ricard Pasanau
owner & enolog

GPS
41.266023
0.841017

Pasanau
La Morera de Montsant, *Carrer de la Bassa*

Visits: Call for information as costs and availability depend upon activities desired.
Contact: 977827202 | informacion@cellerpasanau.com
Website: www.cellerpasanau.com

For those looking to stop in at a cellar upon returning from (most likely not going to) a hike up in the cliffs of Montsant natural park, Pasanau is perfectly located at the top of La Morera. Any visit to the cellar will bear witness to a great number of people strolling up to the trailhead slathered in ropes and other climbing gear. For those who prefer less intense activities, the cellar offers a chance to taste the wines made from the grapes grown right up next to these mountains.

The Pasanau family has always had vines in La Morera, an area that has some llicorella stones but also calcareous soils. But in 1986 they started planting new vines -- including the oldest Cabernet Sauvignon in Priorat which they planted at an altitude of 750m. They were members of the Poboleda cooperative, but decided to start their own winery in 1995. The three Pasanau brothers, with the support of their father, worked together to build the cellar and add one tank at a time to gradually increase their production to the roughly 50,000 bottles a year that they make now. Ricard Pasanau, who holds a masters in viticulture, is the manager and enolog of the winery.

View of vineyards and Priorat

Ceps Nous 2010 sees no barrel aging, but is fermented at a higher temperature for more extraction. It has a light, slight, dusty nose. The body shows the young wine that it is, but with more character. Full and meaty, the acids and tannins are quite present and carry in to the finish.

70% Grenache, 15% Cab Sauv, 10% Merlot, 5% Syrah

 ● | 14,5% | 8-11€

La Morera de Montsant 2006 is much stronger in the nose with immediate dark fruits from the barrel aging. It needs a good hit of decanting to really release everything on offer. The body is deep, but with a large brace of tannins to the back of it. It's a strong bodied wine, but still with a good degree of character. The minerality is present, but different than those at lower altitudes.

52% Grenache, 28% Merlot, 20% Carignan

● | 14,5% | 11-14€

Finca la Planeta 2006 has a generally fat, dark fruit nose. The body carries this, but picks up more of the minerality present and shows the property well from where it's from. It's quite strong bodied but the mineral aspect comes across more like stones after the rain and it stays strong in to the finish. Difficult for all but the largest of meals though. It really starts to develop and round out with more air, taking the edge off of it.

88% Cab Sauvignon, 12% Grenache

● | 14,5% | 16-20€

El Vell Coster 2007 sees 18 months in large French oak barrels and is made from 70 year-old vines. The nose opens with a spicy earthiness that turns in to a rather large body. The minerality comes up more with age as well as a floral touch of violet and licorice. A kick of coffee comes up in the finish, but otherwise lingers out quite pleasantly.

90% Carignan, 10% Grenache

● | 14,5% | 19-25€

Monste Cereceda
owner & enolog

GPS
41.161343
0.716111

La Perla del Priorat
El Molar, *Mas dels Frares*

Visits: Available weekdays with a maximum of 15 people, the cost for a visit and tasting is 6€ per person, but is waived with a purchase of wine.
Contact: 977825202 | frares@laperladelpriorat.com
Website: www.laperladelpriorat.com

There is something eerie about walking around a beautiful hotel that has been closed for some time. It could be that, La Perla del Priorat creates a Catalan setting for "The Shining" or it's just that this property is very, very historic and feels alive with the centuries of people who have visited and lived there. Whichever it is, when asked about the solitude of the estate, the very convivial enologist, Monste Cereceda, who often works late nights in the cellar, prefers to change the subject when it comes up.

This property is one of the oldest in Priorat, having been established in the 15th century as a monastery for the Scala Dei monks. While they had been in their 12th century digs about 30km north for some time, they needed to build this monastery for additional crops and most importantly: wine. The grounds total 102 hectares and while having many other crops, they were heavily planted with vineyards. Originally, the name of the property was, "Mas dels Frares" or "Friars' House", but due to the quality of the wine produced there was changed to "La Perla del Priorat" or "The Pearl of the Priory" sometime back in the 18th century. This makes it one of the oldest wineries in Priorat.

Vineyards

The estate had long been abandoned by the Carthusian monks and the vines killed off by phylloxera when Belgian-Swiss Count Yves Pirenne bought it in 1998 and began replanting vineyards to restart wine production and construct the hotel seen today. It ran for several years successfully in this quite stunning location set amongst the vineyards and up on a quiet hill above the Siurana River with gorgeous views. Due to personal circumstances Count Pirenne had to shut down the hotel. Montse and her business partner, Miquel Sabaté took over the winery portion of La Perla and continue to produce wines from the estate.

Now, from their 22 hectares of vineyards, they produce about 40-50,000 bottles depending on the year. While there is the historical cellar that they've kept as something of a museum, they produce all the wines in the new facilities that were built in the last few years. As to whether or not they'll start aging the wines in the dark, very old, and barely lit catacombs beneath the monastery, Montse again prefers to change the subject.

Bottle archive and cellar

The lower catacombs

Clos les Fites Blanc 2006 has a very mineral nose with tinges of bitter lemon. The body is a rather large departure from this and, while holding a bit of the minerality, is sweet and fruity overall with a freshness that carries in to the finish with a light honey element.
70% Pedro Ximénez, 30% White Grenache

 | 14,5% | 24€

Noster Inicial 2009 has a nose of lighter cherry aromas and an underlying minerality. In the body, all of this pulls together in a consistent wine that's quite agreeable overall and easy to drink. Across the palate, it has a warm texture with pleasant tannins and acids that are balanced in to the finish.
Grenache, Carignan, Cab Sauvignon

 | 15% | 10€

Noster Criança 2008 has aromas of figs and prunes in the nose that float over the top of a mineral base. The body brings up the prune and plum flavors with very nice, tasty tannins. The finish is neutral, fresh, and completes a very nicely constructed wine.
55% Grenache, 45% Carignan
● | 14,5% | 14€ |

Clos les Fites Negre 2006 starts out with a more aggressive nose that, with a touch of decanting lets on its cocoa undertones. The body is plush, enveloping, and brings up hints of black pepper, watercress, and touch of tar that comes up at the finish which, despite the overall strength, clears out quickly with just a pinch of herbal spiciness hanging on.
55% Grenache, 35% Carignan, 10% Cab Sauvignon
● | 15% | 20€

Comte Pirenne 2002 has an initially potent head of aromas despite the 10 years in the bottle, but it quickly blows off to reveal a very nicely structured wine with elegant minerality and tannins throughout the composition of the nose. The body picks up on these elements and expands, revealing a rich, succulent body full of dark fruits, prunes, and only a touch of minerality. The finish comes up concisely and immediately, letting only the best flavors linger on.
55% Grenache, 30% Carignan, 15% Cab Sauvignon
● | 14,5% | 60€ | ✹

LA PERLA DEL PRIORAT

GPS
41.15696
0.784823

Pinord Mas Blanc

Falset, *Carretera Falset-Bellmunt, km 3.5*

Visits: They offer regular winery visits during the week and weekend mornings that cost 7€ including a tasting of their wines. Once or twice a month they also host special activities in the vineyard or tasting classes at 10-15€ a person. Call or visit their website for more information and to make reservations.
Contact: 938903066 | pinord@pinord.es
Website: www.pinord.com
Languages: English, French, German

The Pinord name is not a new one to the wine world. The Tetas family has been producing wines up in Penedès for over 150 years, setting up their own winery in 1942. The company's name comes from one of their original vineyards in Penedès, known as "Pi del Nord" (pine of the North in Catalan). Since then, their winery has kept on growing and continuously offering new wines--including their famous Reynal frizzante or naturally sparkling wines. In the 1990s, the family wanted to expand beyond their native Penedès and diversify their portfolio. Thus, in 1999 they purchased the semi-abandoned Mas Blanc on the road from Falset to Bellmunt and started planting 18 hectares of vineyards. This endeavor took them a couple of years due to terracing of the land. In 2002 they produced their first vintage in Priorat.

From that very first vintage, their wines have been certified as organic. Additionally, in 2007 they became the first winery not just in Priorat or Catalonia, but in all of Spain to receive the strict Demeter biodynamic certification.

With all of these systems in place and paying a great deal of respect to the environment where they are producing, they manage to make about 50,000 bottles a year. Of course, this pales in comparison to the parent winery's five million liters a year produced up in Penedès, which is the same amount as all the wineries in the DOQ Priorat appellation combined.

Clos del Mas 2008 has sage and mineral elements in the nose, and a nice deep color. The body has red berry aromas and is immediately approachable, with a degree of freshness and contained acidity for good meal pairings despite being rather strong in tannins. Acidity lingers in to finish but cleans up well and would be great for everyday drinking.
Cab Sauvignon, Carignan, Grenache
🔴 | 14,5% | 12-15€

+7 2008 is named after the sun orientations of the vineyards. It has elements of vanilla and cake bread to the nose. There are large tannins in to the body, but still generally smooth across the palate. The acidity is downplayed, but would still work well with many meals. Overall, a classic Priorat wine.
50% Grenache, 50% Cab Sauvignon/Syrah
🔴 | 15% | 18-25€

Clos del Músic 2008 really lets the slate soil come through in the nose. Mineral elements come up as well. It's larger on the palate with stronger tannins and brings up leather elements as it decants and hangs around a good deal in to the finish.
Cab Sauvignon, Grenache, Merlot, Syrah
🔴 | 14,5% | 23-30€

Balcons 2006 is named as a tribute to the older terraces that are like balconies. The nose is dark, smoky with elements of tar and a good dose of currant. It has a nice kick of acidity that eventually works in to a tart finish. It sticks across the finish and lingers a great deal.
Cab Sauvignon, Carignan, Grenache, Merlot
🔴 | 14,5% | 25-31€

PINORD MAS BLANC

Down the same road as Domini de la Cartoixa, just south of El Molar there sits Pins Vers. Named after the type of Mediterranean pines that produce edible nuts, the winery was founded in 2002 by a few partners including Fina Escoda and Josep Anguera, whose father owned vineyards in the area. For years they were selling their grapes off to the local collective but decided to start making their own wines and eventually constructed their cellar in 2004, also producing their first vintage that year.

All told, they currently have 5.5 hectares of vineyards with 50 year-old Carignan and 15-25 year-old Grenache, Cabernet Sauvignon and Syrah. The soils in this southern region are a mix of llicorella and sedimentary, which include calcareous materials, clay, river pebbles, and eroded slate.

One of the co-owners, Montse Nadal who also teaches at the University of Tarragona's viticulture and enology program, is the enolog.

Jaume Anguera
owner

GPS
41.155099
0.710999

Pins Vers

El Molar, *Camí de la Solana*

Visits: They can welcome a maximum of 20 people to visit the cellar and have a tasting. Call or email for pricing and reservations.
Contact: 977825458, 680484167 | info@lafuina.com
Website: www.lafuina.com
Languages: English, French

Els Pins Vers 2008 sees 15 months in French oak. The nose brings up the typical Priorat elements of dark fruits and minerality. The body is a pleasant expression, being light across the palate and quite well balanced with well constructed tannins in the finish.
70% Grenache, 20% Carignan, 5% Cab Sauv, 5% Syrah
● | 15% | 14€

La Fuina 2006 is named after the marten and is also the name given by locals to one of the vineyards. It sees 12 months of barrel aging. It has more elaborated aspects to the nose and body that show the oak aging. The mineral aspects take on more of a granitic tone that takes time to bring out by decanting.
40% Grenache, 40% Cab Sauvignon, 20% Carignan
● | 14% | 16€

PINS VERS

The Piñol i Sabaté family has a long history as vine growers in Priorat, with vineyards in both El Lloar and El Molar. In one they have Grenache and Cabernet and in the other they have old Carignan. They started making their own wine in 2007 and for a few harvests now they've been working to make what they consider to be a true expression of Priorat, that shows their love of the land. At the center of their winemaking philosophy is the grape, which they like to pick when it's at its best and select only the best fruits both in the vineyard and in the selection table at the cellar.

They currently make 10,000 bottles of the Sirona, which is a non-aged younger style of wine, and 5,000 bottles of the Neix9 that spends 12-18 months in French and Hungarian oak barrels.

Carles Piñol
owner

Piñol i Sabaté
El Lloar / El Molar

Visits: Not currently open for public visits
Contact: 608269093 | info@pinyolsabate.com
Website: www.pinyolsabate.com

Sirona 2008 puts out a nose of red cherry and raspberry. It's overall neutral and initially spicy with a blueberry undertone and develops a dusty texture. It gets a bit rustic and burly as it sees more air.
70% Cab Sauvignon, 30% Grenache/Carignan
● | 14,5% | 13-14€

Neix9 2007 initially shows a dark fruit nose with light, aromatic spices to it. Dark cherry and red plum are found in the body and the spiciness continues in a light form. It develops large tannins and the finish is dry with lingering acidity. It gets earthy as it breathes with a generally sweet aspect and while it grows in overall size and fatness, it then mellows out to present a very approachable wine.
60% Grenache, 40% Cab Sauvignon/Carignan
● | 14,3% | 22-24€

A group of friends with ties to Priorat, including owning vineyards around La Vilella Baixa, decided to form Celler del Pont in 1998. In total, they have about five hectares of vines with about half of them younger vines at around 20 years old. The other half is comprised of old vines with more than 50 years. They produce about 7,000 bottles of their one wine Lo Givot in a good harvest year along with 500 bottles of a limited-edition dessert wine some years. As this wine is a labor of love, they continue selling grapes to other wineries.

The cellar is a compact operation, set under one of the older homes in the village. Just outside the front cellar is the 18th century, Pont de Pedra which is an old, Romanesque stone bridge that spans the Montsant River, linking the village to its residents' gardens. Naturally, the winery takes its name from this bridge in this beautiful and tranquil corner of the village.

Sisco Fernandez
owner

GPS
41.219433
0.762914

Celler del Pont
La Vilella Baixa, *Carrer del Riu, 1*

Visits: Not currently open for public visits
Contact: 977828231,650726440 | cellerdelpont@gmail.com
Website: www.cellerdelpont.com

Lo Givot 2008 brings up a red berry nose with aromas of cherry and crème. It's a slightly different style than other similar reds given that the body is a touch sweet but still holds plenty of acidity to push through meals. Balanced overall, it lets on just the smallest touch of oak in a very approachable wine.

33% Grenache, 33% Carignan, 24% Cab Sauvignon, 10% Syrah

● | 14,8% | 30€

Born of a family tradition in wine, Prior Pons was established in 2000 by Jou Escoda, Emili Mayo and Toni Coca and had its first vintage in 2002. Prior to that, Jou's father was making bulk wine on a small, familial scale, selling it in Reus and Navarra, and even bottling it for a while back in 1960. In the 1980s he stopped making wine and sold his grapes to others, including, Mas Alta. Their old stone family house of Ca la Ponça in La Vilella Alta is from the 18th century and is where they started production over a decade ago, making some 2,300 bottles a for their first vintage. Also, Prior Pons is named after the house.

With Toni Coca as the enologist, they quickly increased their profile as a high quality winery. They now make about 15,000 bottles a year and recently moved to the old cellar of the cooperative in El Lloar. However, they still make their two wines from their 10 hectares of vineyards in La Vilella Alta which are all owned by Jou's family. Their oldest vineyards are of Carignan grapes, planted in 1946 in the Cabanet and Les Planes properties. Their youngest are of Cabernet Sauvignon planted on the L'Espitlla property in 1995. Additionally, they have two more plots planted in 2003 that they haven't started using yet.

Jou Escoda
owner

GPS
41.186894
0.748416

Prior Pons

El Lloar, *Carrer Masons, La Coopertiva Agrícola*

Visits: Not currently open for public visits
Contact: 606547865, 608251303 | info@priorpons.com
Website: www.priorpons.com

Planets 2009 opens up jammy and thick in the nose initially with a great wealth of dark fruits. The body brings these fruits up more alongside spicy peppery notes and a hint of licorice. It is tasty and thick on the palate. The finish carries out smoothly.
40% Grenache, 40% Carignan, 10% Cab Sauvignon, 5% Merlot, 5% Syrah

● | 14.5% | 10-15€ | ⚖ | ✸

Prior Pons 2009 is a bit tight upon first opening, but still shows cloves and minerality. After decanting for an hour, the body equalizes a great deal and shows dark fruits along with a smooth buttery aspect and expanded minerality. The acids grow and the wine develops in to a fine, complex elaboration.
45% Carignan, 40% Grenache, 15% Cab Sauvignon

● | 15% | 26-30€

Sílvia Puig
owner & enolog

GPS
41.188989
0.78522

Puig Priorat

Gratallops, *Carretera Falset-Gratallops, km 8*

Visits: They welcome guests on a limited basis. Call for availability or to buy wines directly.
Contact: 977054032, 681114271 | mail@puigpriorat.com
Website: www.puigpriorat.com
Languages: English

Up on a hill, just before you enter Gratallops and facing west, sits what looks like a small red church. To first-time visitors it might seem that this is the Mare de Déu de la Consolació hermitage, but that's actually on the other side of the village. Closer inspection will reveal that this "church" has what seems like an odd mix of different historical icons about it and is not a church at all, but the wine cellar of Puig Priorat, also known as Ithaca.

In 1998, the Puig family of Penedès bought the land around the cellar due to their friendship with René Barbier. After a long process of terracing the land, they began planting in 2000. Initially they were making wines with grapes they bought from other growers in a small cabin in the middle of the vineyards with difficult access. But, things became a bit easier once they finished building their modern cellar in 2003. The Greek references they ended up basing the wines around was due to Joseph Puig and his daughter Sílvia (now the enolog) being fascinated with the fact that the Greeks were the ones responsible for originally bringing wine to the Iberian Peninsula.

Over a decade after starting they now have 14 hectares of their own vineyards that they harvest from and produce about 40,000 bottles a year, the majority of which they export. They are probably the only winery in Priorat that focuses a large part of their production on white wines which Sílvia admits was a challenge since most white vines in Priorat were ripped out in the 1990s. They also make an atypical dessert wine made with Hairy Grenache.

Akyles Blanc 2011 is made with young Macabeu vines. It has a fresh nose with citric aromas and an underlying minerality that's unusual for this varietal. The body picks up on this and is refreshing with a bright acidity that pushes through in to the finish.
100% Macabeu

 | 13,5% | 12€

Odysseus Garnatxa Blanca 2011 is fresh in the nose with an interesting aspect of soft cantaloupe. The body departs from the nose a bit with a more white pepper quality to it and general spiciness that fills out the palate and picks up in to the finish with some floral notes. It's a well-structured white that would pair well with meat as well as grilled fish.
100% White Grenache

 | 14,5% | 14€ |

Akyles Negre 2009 is a very food-friendly wine. The nose is primarily red fruits with a touch of underlying minerality. The body picks up more black pepper and anise elements to it that carry out in to a more tannic finish that comes up fresh.
45% Carignan, 40% Hairy Grenache, 15% Cab Sauv

 | 15% | 15€ |

Odysseus Negre 2009 gives a nose with richer, more succulent dark fruits and more defined minerality. The body brings up spicy dark cherry flavors with a buttery, smooth texture that carries out in to the finish which leaves a pleasing acidity and can age well for 2-3 more years.
40% Grenache, 40% Carignan, 20% "Others"

 | 15% | 28€

Odysseus Maset del Ros 2007 is a limited, selected wine of about 2,000 bottles a year. The nose is dark and deep with touches of smokiness and licorice. This translates well in to the body. The minerality comes up and makes for a more bold wine that would happily stand up to game dishes.
40% Grenache/Hairy Grenache, 22% Carignan, 20% Syrah, 18% Cab Sauvignon

 | 15% | 38-40€

PUIG PRIORAT

Ricard Rofes is the enolog and manager at the Scala Dei winery and in between his time spent aging and blending the harvests, he has been producing his line of RAR wines since 2008. His tagline for these is, "Vins Singulars" which, while it could be taken that they're wines of singular and stunning quality it has more to do with the unique nature of the project.

While Rofes has no vines of his own, each year, he has worked to select special vineyards in Priorat to buy the grapes and make a wine that showcases that locale as much as it can. Interestingly, he started making a white with old-vine White Grenache grapes from La Macipa property up in the Montsant mountains at 650m of altitude.

RAR Blanc 3 2010 opens with a good burst of minerality and oak elements to the nose. Given a bit of time decanting, the oak blows off to some degree and becomes more integrated with the rest of the wine. While strong and bold, it still gives up a good degree of fruit. The finish brings out a touch of acidity.
80% White Grenache, 20% Chenin Blanc

 | 14,5% | 29€

Ricard Rofes
owner & enolog

GPS
41.248191
0.811239

RAR
Escaladei

Visits: Not currently open for public visits
Website: www.vinssingulars.com

Raret 2011 has a nose that opens with fantastic, well defined dark chocolate and coffee aromas. The body loses a good deal of this and picks up a more fresh character, although it remains brooding and dark, initially not letting on the youth of the wine. The finish cleans out everything incredibly fast.
100% Grenache
● | 14,5% | 10-11€

RAR Negre 4 2010 has a sultry and dark berry nose. Touches of minerality grow in it with air. The body is light and a touch spicy. It's full of the locale and the definitive Grenache qualities found there. The finish is soft on the palate and lingers with spice. As it decants, a chocolate aspect comes in as well as earthiness that play out effortlessly.
100% Grenache
● | 14,5% | 29€ |

Marc Ripoll Sans
owner & enolog

GPS
41.194592
0.777867

🍷

Ripoll Sans

Gratallops, *Carrer Baixada Consolació, 4*

Visits: They welcome 2-10 people at a cost of 10€ per person for a taste of the wines and visit of the cellar, mostly on weekends but call ahead to see about their availability.
Contact: 687638951 | mripoll@closabatllet.com
Website: www.facebook.com/closabatllet

Besides having a long tradition of viticulture in the family, Marc Ripoll Sans' grandfather had been growing grapes that he sold to the local cooperative and had even made his own wines for a brief period during the 1960s. Marc decided to start his own winery in the Cal Batllet family house in 2000, which was also the year of their first vintage. It was a smaller production of 7,000 bottles that was made only with the best selection of their grapes. It apparently proved promising as they continued to grow and eventually reached about 22,000 bottles a year in their attractive old cellar with vaulted ceilings on the north side of the village of Gratallops.

One of those who are passionate about the region their wines come from, Marc is a staunch supporter of traditional local Priorat grapes. For instance, he is the only one to produce a 100% Escanya-Vella wine. This is an old white grape that's found in dwindling numbers these days, possibly in part to the name meaning "old lady strangler" or just in part to the preference given to foreign grapes. He also has old Carignan vines that's he's very fond of and finds Gratallops to be the perfect environment for these varietal. In showing devotion to the land, all his vines are certified organic and all of his wines have the "Vi de la Vila" certification.

Escanya-Vella 2010 is made from this native white grape that has a thick skin and high acidity with only 600 bottles made per year. It has a most curious nose with touches of f and slight floral elements mixed with an un dertone of citric qualities. The body depa from this a great deal and is surprisingly lig. across the palate and easy to drink with a tiny touch of minerality coming up as it breathes. It has a well defined acidity that carries the wine well along in to the finish.
100% Escanyavella

 | 13,5% | 16-18€ |

Artai 2009 is a blend from their younger vines named after Marc's two year-old son. The nose is full of dark berries and a defining undercurrent of the oak despite only a portion of it being aged in barrels. These aromas and construction carry in to the body a good deal, but it adds spiciness and a roundness that grabs you and carries to the finish.
50% Grenache, 25% Carignan, 20% Cab Sauvignon, 5% Syrah

● | 15% | 11-13€ | 🏛 | ⚖ | ✹

5 Partides 2009 is a blend of up to 100 year old Carignan vines from 5 different small plots, and only 2,600 bottles are produced every year. It presents a lovely, slightly glowing purple in the glass. It has a nose full of buttery and interesting mineral qualities. It's fermented in new, open top barrels and then later aged in them as well. It is a deep and complex wine, full of character from the village. The aromas translate very well in to the body and add in dark spice flavors such as blackcurrants. The finish lingers a bit, picking up on the strength of the body.
100% Carignan

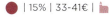

● | 15% | 33-41€ | 🏛

Torroja Ronçavall 2009 is a tribute to Marc's mother who was from Torroja del Priorat. This wine is made with grapes from a single Carignan vineyard that her father planted some 75 years ago. It is fermented in new open-top barrels and then aged in them for 15 months. They only make a super-limited production of 269 bottles a year.
100% Carignan

● | 15% | 75€ | 🏛

RIPOLL SANS

There is a sheer cliff on the Montsant bluff that reaches over 1,100 meters in height. As it is straight up and down, once there was no shadow on it anymore, historically, the locals would know that it was the middle of the day and head home for lunch. Nearly right up against this natural sundial, Roca de les Dotze has their property of 45 hectares and has taken the name from it which means "Noon Rock". Parts of their 13ha of vineyards, which are at 700 meters, reside in the Parc Natural del Montsant.

Enric Henry and Lourdes Rispa are wine lovers who always been interested in Priorat. So in 1999 they purchased this property and started working on it, building terraces and planting vineyards. After a couple of test vintages, in 2006 they produced their first actual vintage. All their vineyards are certified organic and they have solar panels to operate machinery and pumps. They have a project to build a full-fledged winery at some point in the future within their estate, but meanwhile they are using the facilities of another winery in Escaladei to make their wine. They currently produce about 10,000 bottles a year between their two labels, with Josep Serra taking care of the enology.

Enric Henry
Lourdes Rispa
owners

GPS
41.2719
0.870505

Roca de les Dotze
Escaladei

Visits: Not currently open for public visits
Contact: 662302214 | info@rocadelesdotze.cat
Website: www.rocadelesdotze.cat

Noray 2007 has a touch of mineral components mixed in to a dark fruit nose. The body carries the minerality and tosses up hints of the slate. It rounds out well and shows good integration as it breathes with red fruits on the finish as well as a good deal of coffee elements coming up.
60% Grenache, 20% Cab Sauvignon, 10% Carignan, 10% Syrah

 | 14% | 15€

Roca Bruixa 2007 has a dark berry nose with dark hints of fennel and caraway seeds. There is a light dose of acidity to the body as well as slight leather and clay aspect. The acidity sticks in to the finish and pulls up a little red fruit on the finish.
75% Grenache, 25% Syrah

 | 14% | 27€

Albert Rotllan Torra
owner

GPS
41.213293
0.810024

Rotllan Torra
Torroja del Priorat, *Carrer Balandra, 6*

Visits: The price is 8€ per person for a two hour visit and tasting.
Contact: 977839285 | comercial@rotllantorra.com
Website: rotllantorra.com

The old cellar of Rotllan Torra lays claim to a good deal of history. It dates back to about 400 years ago, with impressive high vaulted ceilings that were typical at the time. Apparently the Carthusian monks built it in the 17th century and they built it with large intentions. At its maximum, it could produce one million liters of wine, although this function was largely forgotten during the Spanish Civil War when it was used as a stable. They still conserve a 200L chestnut wine tank, though, which has been converted into a small tasting room.

The Rotllan Torra family, who worked in the wine distribution business, visited Torroja while on vacation and fell in love with it. So in 1982 they bought the cellar and began producing their first wines in 1984 when there were only four or five wineries producing bottled wines in Priorat. Now they own 25 hectares of vineyards and buy from 25 more to produce nearly 100,000 bottles a year. While a great deal less than the heyday of this historical cellar, it's still a healthy amount for the region.

A "wine study" inside an enormous, old barrel

Rotllan Torra Criança 2009 has a light, subtle nose with hints of blackberry and dark fruits and mineral aspects, but generally easygoing. The body is stronger with more of a brace of tannins to it, but not over the top. Mineral components come up more with decanting as well as stony fruits. The finish comes up strong and holds on for a bit.
Grenache, Carignan, Cab Sauvignon
● | 13.5% | 8€

Rotllan Torra Reserva 2008 has a richer nose that frames the mineral elements of the land quite well. The body is surprising as it brings up a lot of red fruit elements and the minerality is downplayed. The finish then pulls up quite light with slight, lingering dried fruits.
Grenache, Cab Sauvignon, Carignan
● | 13.5% | 10€

Tirant 2008 has a blackberry and roasted hazelnut nose with touch of burnt caramel to it. The minerality is largely downplayed with dark fruits being the focus that carries in to the finish with a touch of bitter chocolate.
Carignan, Grenache, Cab Sauvignon, Syrah, Merlot
● | 15.5% | 42€

Moscatell has a fresh, stony nose like a mountain stream just after the rain has touched it. Small hints of almonds and hazelnuts come up with air. The body is wonderfully light and dances across the palate. It lightly warms the throat on the finish. It's an extremely articulate dessert wine of which they only make about 2,000 bottles.
100% Moscatell
 | 16% | 8.50€

Jaume Sabaté
owner

GPS
41.22072
0.763268

Sabaté
La Vilella Baixa, *Carrer Nou, 6*

Visits: They offer a visit of their two cellars and a taste free of charge with a minimum of four people. They prefer for people to call ahead for reservations if possible, although a taste of their wines can be had at their shop without notice. Their hours are Monday to Saturday from 9-14h and 16-19h and Sundays from 9-14h.
Contact: 977839209 | cellersabate@cellersabate.com
Website: www.cellersabate.com

Situated in the center of La Vilella Baixa, Celler Sabaté is an old family winery and shop that has its foundations in 1910 although it's probably older. They were either the second or third cellar to be established in Priorat. Their shop is conveniently located along the main street in town next to the butcher selling Priorat's famous llonganissa sausages. In addition to selling all of their bottled wines, they also sell them in bulk and they have a good selection of local food products in the region, including fruits and vegetables from their garden. And it needs to be mentioned that they have nut and olive trees to make their own delicious olive oil.

Until 20 years ago the Sabaté cellar was located where their shop is now, but these days they produce in a larger space nearby. It's a warehouse full of modern tanks and barrels where they produce about 30,000 bottles a year. Then there's the antique cellar by the river where they have their old barrels, and is kept more for the history than anything else although they still have a small amount of "vi ranci" that they make there. Although the Sabaté son, Jaume studied enology and is actively involved in the winemaking

Their old family cellar

process, Roser Amorós who also advises a number of wineries in the region, consults with them.

Their grapes all come from their 28 hectares of vineyards and they make 25-30,000 bottles a year with them. Their wines are sold under the brand Mas Plantadeta, which is the name of their main property. Unlike most other wineries in Priorat who rely heavily on exports, Sabaté's wines are sold mainly at their shop in La Vilella or at Vinateria Tot Vi that they also own in Reus.

Blanc 2011 has a relatively fruity nose with easy elements to it. The body is smooth and easy to kick back with a small bit of acidity to make it happily pair with foods.
100% White Grenache
 | 13.5% | 6-8€

Negre 2010 has a light nose that's not terrible complex, but is easy to drink. The body is sweeter than most wines in the region. Rather large tannins through the body and in to the finish.
100% Grenache
 | 14.5% | 9-10€

Criança 2006 has a naturally more complex nose that carries in to a more structure, defined body that drops the sweetness seen in the younger wines and brings up more tar and bitter chocolate elements.
50% Grenache, 25% Cab Sauvignon, 25% Carignan
 | 14.5% | 13€

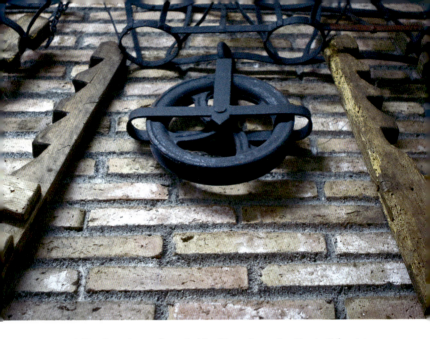

A family winery founded by Torroja native Enric Sabaté i Vendrell and his two sons Enric and Josep Maria Sabaté i Franquet , they planted their vines about 12 years ago to start making traditional Priorat wines. They had their first harvest in 2009 and now produce about 14,000 bottles a year from their two hectares of vineyards.

Their cellar is set on the northeast side of Torroja, just up the street from the local bus stop, a few steps away from Llicorella Vins, and they produce all the wine from their two historic properties known locally as "Cal Rouer" and "Cal Senyor Antón". Their enolog is Montse Cereceda of La Perla del Priorat. In addition to the two labels that they release, they are also working on a "vi ranci" for sale at some point in the future.

Enric Sabaté
owner

GPS
41.213644
0.811234

Sabaté Franquet
Torroja del Priorat, *Carrer de l'Era, 25*

Visits: There is no cost for visits, but prior reservation by phone is required.
Contact: 977839337 | cellersabatefranquet@hotmail.com
Website: www.cellersabate.com

Sybaris 2011 is bright in the glass and easy to drink, holding back its 15% strength of alcohol quite well. It's slightly herbal and mineral in the nose with hints of red berries in the body. The finish is fresh, clean, and approachable.

Grenache, Carignan, Cab Sauvignon

● | 15% | 6€ |

Berta 2010 has a nose with more pronounced herbal and mineral notes that focus around sage elements. In the body there is a touch of clay to it, but it is light overall. The finish is dry, but brings up sweet touches of licorice and a neutral acidity that rounds out a bit with decanting.

Grenache, Carignan, Cab Sauvignon

● | 15% | 10€ |

The family of Jordi Sabaté is originally from Torroja but like many they moved to Barcelona decades ago as prior to the new age of wine in Priorat, village life was extremely hard. Jordi however studied enology and decided to start making wine again in the cellar under his family's house. In 2000, they planted new vines in their vineyard of about three hectares. In 2004, they finished rehabilitating the cellar, which included a great deal of reinforcement as a section that is under one of the streets had collapsed. That year they also made the first vintage and are currently producing only 7,000 bottles annually.

Jordi has had some bumps along the way such as the DOQ body rejecting the name of his popular entry level wine, "Dos Borratxos" as it means, "Two Drunks". Featuring an illustration by cartoonist Enric Rebollo (aka Joso) on the label, it was meant to appeal to a younger crowd. Also, his Vertical wine is essentially a "Vi de la Vila" wine, but Jordi didn't want to go through the certification process and thus writes "Vi de Poble" on the label.

While the cellar isn't technically open for public visits, Jordi's friendliness makes it something of the local Torroja winemaker hangout on weekends.

José María Pérez
Jordi Sabaté
assistant, owner & enolog

GPS
41.214417
0.810091

Sabaté i Mur
Torroja del Priorat, *Carrer Major, 47*

Visits: Not currently open for public visits
Contact: 677354167 | jsabateroig@gmail.com

Dos Borratxos 2010 is an immediately approachable wine with touches of dark fruits and minerality. These transfer in to the body and pick up a touch of tar and dry prunes come out in the finish. As it breathes, the whole wine softens a great deal and in general it's a wonderful wine for all types of drinkers and pairs well with many dishes.
90% Grenache, 10% Cab Sauvignon

● | 14.5% | 12-14€ | |

Vertical 2005 has soft dark and red fruits to the nose that take on a dusty, blueberry quality. The tannins and acids come up in the body with a balance and strong minerality. The finish is clean and bright with more red fruits developing as it decants. It's a lovely craft wine with a very limited production that seems to be able to age for more years.
100% Carignan

● | 14.5% | 35-38€

Pere Sangenís
owner

GPS
41.187647
0.856697

Sangenís i Vaqué

Porrera, *Plaça Catalunya, 3*

Visits: They welcome people every day at a cost of 6€ per person for a visit and tasting. Call for reservations.
Contact: 977828238, 977828252 | celler@sangenisivaque.com
Website: www.sangenisivaque.com
Languages: English, French

While winemaking runs deep and in the family histories of Pere Sangenís and Conxita Vaqué, it has started and stopped at various points throughout the decades. It wasn't until 1978 when the two of them created their winery and planted vines on the Monlleó property that has been in Pere's family since at least 1700. In 1979, they started producing wines at the same cellar they're using today on Plaça Catalunya in Porrera. This cellar was from Conxita's family and her grandfather Josep Simó had actually been making wine in it starting the late 19th century.

Now, the daughters, María and Núria have joined in the enology alongside their father. Pere is very proud of them but admits to being a demanding head of the family, always striving to be better. They harvest from 13ha around the area and produce one white, five reds, and a sweet, although the later only has a 400 bottle release. Their cellar, while initially having a very warehouse appearance, gets more intimate and interesting in the upper floors where they have a classy barrel room full of excellent wines awaiting their turn to be drank.

Sangenís i Vaqué Porrera 2008 is made without any oak aging. It has a light nose with a hint of acidity. The acidity kicks up a bit more in the bottle and minerality is introduced showing the soil character. Overall it has quite an easygoing character.
45% Grenache, 45% Carignan, 10% Syrah

 | 14.5% | 9€

Dara 2008 presents a nose with dark fruit aromas as well as a hint of sweet beeswax to it. The body has a small degree of minerality, but is more acidic than others of this blend. Good fruits in that it doesn't overwhelm, but is rather light in character with a pleasant dusting of chocolate to the finish.
50% Grenache, 50% Carignan

 | 15% | 11€

Vall Por 2004 is the original name for Porerra. The nose has initially strong oak aromas that blow off quickly with air and then it presents soft tobacco and chocolate aromas with a hint of dried fig. The body is much stronger than others with larger tannins and stickiness across the palate. Despite this strength, it finishes out quite quickly.

30% Grenache, 30% Carignan, 15% Cab Sauvignon, 15% Merlot, 10% Syrah

 | 15% | 14€

Coranya 2004 gives off a nose that's warmer with enjoyable mineral elements to it that show the property from which it takes its name. There is larger minerality in the body that sits very nicely in the mouth. Some herbaceous elements come up as it breaths, but overall it has an aspect of being earthy and tasting the soil with hints of root vegetables, but not green in any way. Has a finish that lingers with a pleasing freshness.

50% Grenache, 50% Carignan

 | 14.5% | 27€

Clos Monlleó 2000 has dark berry aspects that come up in the nose quickly. Succulent and deep, the aromas are something to get lost in. The body is full and compliments the nose, but is still very well balanced with acids and tannins reigned in and nothing overwhelming. The berries of the nose come up in the flavors, especially blackberry. Mineral qualities are downplayed a little in favor of larger spicy elements like cassis and cardamom. The finish comes up plush.

50% Grenache, 50% Carignan

 | 15% | 42€

Fredi Torres
owner & enolog

GPS
41.1932
0.77828

Saó de Coster
Gratallops, *Carrer dels Valls, 8*

Visits: They only conduct them in a limited fashion depending on their availability, and prior reservations via phone or email are required. It costs 10€ a person for a visit to the vineyards, cellar and tasting.
Contact: 977839298, 650284753 | info@saodelcoster.com
Website: www.saodelcoster.com
Languages: English, French

It's oft forgotten in winemaking these days, but at its core, it is an agricultural endeavor that requires getting one's hands dirty and being in tune with the land from which the grapes come. Within 10 seconds of a first encounter with Fredi Torres, you see that he not only remembers this, but lives it daily.

Originally from Galicia in Spain, Fredi grew up in Switzerland and spent the first part of his adult life traveling the world as a DJ until he found a new calling: wine. He worked four vintages in Argentina when eventually he found his way to Priorat about 10 years ago. He was, to put it mildly, enchanted and glows when speaks of the rugged landscape, the llicorella soils, and the natural beauty as elements that all called to him. After spending so many years working indoors in clubs, he's now happy to spend his days out in the vineyards.

While many see a land such as this and set about to carve new terraces in to the hills and mountains, Fredi preferred a more difficult and holistic approach. He's been working for the last decade to recuperate vineyards that are quite old and have been left to whither and eventually die. It's not a project for the faint of heart as he uses biodynamic methods, no herbicides or pesticides and plows all of the vineyards and their crumbly slate soils with mules. His original mule Morena, now an old lady, worked for 14 years on Álvaro Palacios' famous L'Ermita vineyard. She helped Fredi start as he found her to have a Swiss precision in her abilities. Her younger replacement, Pepe apparently is still on a learning curve.

With a large personal effort, mule power, and dedication, Fredi and his team have taken six hectares (that all seem to slant upwards at 45 degrees) with vines that were barely producing 300 grams of grapes apiece to the point where they now produce 20,000 bottles a year. After all, the name of the winery in Catalan means something along the lines of, "the fertile soil on the slopes".

S 2010 only sees aging in stainless tanks and no oak barrels with a label that's designed by Fredi's brother. It's herbaceous and full of character in the nose. The body is chewy and tasty with fig, carob and flavors of caramel. It really opens up nicely as it breathes and is a well-suited wine for everyday drinking.

30% Grenache, 25% Cab Sauv, 25% Merlot, 20% Syrah

● | 14,5% | 12€ |

Terram 2009 opens with an elegant and subtle sweetness, cocoa and cloves in the nose. Although it spends four years in French oak barrels, half of them new, it doesn't overpower the aromas in the body. It has a surprisingly large acidity to it and spicy notes. The lingering finish carries its acidity and tannins, leaving a note of fennel at the very end.

40% Grenache, 45% Cab Sauvignon, 15% Syrah

● | 14% | 25€

Canyarets 2008 is composed of Carignan from 85 year-old vines and is only the finest selection of the harvest's grapes. It has a subtle, dusty nose, and a really well balanced body that continues to open and grow as it decants. While it spends four years in used barrels, you don't taste it at all as the oak is aligned perfectly to add complexity without being overbearing. It shows how exquisite and wonderful Carignan can become when the vines are old.

100% Carignan

● | 13% | 80€ |

SAÓ DE COSTER

Sara Pérez and René Barbier IV are both the children of pioneers of the 1990s Priorat revolution, and both have taken over their world-renowned family wineries. With such weight on their shoulders it's only natural that they felt like starting their own project together and in 2002 they bought a very steep, old vineyard in Gratallops named, Bellvisos.

René says that after 10 years working in his family winery mainly in the cellar, he felt the need to work outdoors and converse with the vines. The Bellvisos vineyard is in the middle of a forest with trees and other plants mixed in between the vines, and it was abandoned before the introduction of herbicides of pesticides. So working with this vineyard they realized the importance of crop diversity and harmony with the environment which led to plowing with mules and applying biodynamic agriculture methods.

When they first bought the vineyard they thought it was all Carignan but it turned out to be half Hairy Grenache, which makes the Bellvisos wine quite fresh and unique. They also make a white Bellvisos and a young red with newer vines planted in the property called, Partida Pedrer. They make all their wines with natural yeasts and, as of 2012, without adding sulfites.

René Barbier IV
Sara Pérez
Leo Barbier Pérez
owners & enologs, future

GPS
41.198613
0.795411

Sara i René Viticultors
Gratallops

Visits: If you find yourself visiting Clos Mogador you can find bottles of their wines and René Barbier IV is more than happy to talk about this project with visitors.
Contact: rene@venuslauniversal.com
Website: www.venuslauniversal.com/#sara_i_rene

Blanc 2010 is a full-bodied white wine made with old vine White Grenache and Macabeu that grow at the top and bottom of the property. It has wild herb aromas and a darker yellow color that is the result of maceration with the skins and fermentation in a 600L barrel. Less than 1,000 bottles made a year.
White Grenache, Macabeu

 | 14% | 39€

Negre 2006 is fermented in 300L open barrels with natural yeasts, and the wine is then aged for up to 20 months in the same barrels. It has a nose that is buttery with dark fruit and a meaty aspect like rare beef. The body is rich and voluptuous, loving on the palate, but strong and earnest, full of licorice and earthiness that carry in to the finish.
Hairy Grenache, Carignan

 | 14% | 45€ | ✹

Ricard Rofes
manager & enolog

GPS
41.248191
0.811239

Cellers de Scala Dei
Escaladei, *Rambla Cartoixa*

Visits: Their tasting room is open weekdays from 12-17:00 and weekends from 10:30-18:00 with tastings ranging 6-10€ per person. Full winery tours are conducted daily by one of the Mestres brothers, in multiple languages and for groups of maximum 50 people, but it's advisable to call for specific times and to book.
Contact: 977827027 | info@cellersdescaladei.com
Website: www.grupocodorniu.com
Languages: English, French

While there are a core group of wineries that brought fame to Priorat some 25 years ago, it was Cellers de Scala Dei that was in part responsible for bringing the "famemakers" to Priorat. Once refounded in 1973, it was the first winery showing the world that consistently high quality, modern wines could be produced from Priorat. Of course, their complete history goes back much, much further.

Scala Dei owes its foundation to the Carthusian monks from France that set up shop in the area in the 12th century, building their monastery just up the road from where the village now sits. While it seems viticulture existed in the area, the monks brought more refined techniques and gradually increased the production of wine in the area which thrived until the Ecclesiastical Confiscations of 1835. At that point a few wealthy families purchased the monastery and its properties and established the Unión de Scala Dei. They started bottling high quality wines in the 1870s as a private enterprise, as shown by their silver medal in 1978 Paris World's Fair, thus laying the foundations for the modern winery there today. Eventually it was dissolved and the partners divided the properties among themselves.

Barrel cellar

With phylloxera and the Spanish Civil war, the winery entered a decline during the first half of the 20th century. In the 1960s the descendant of one of the Scala Dei owners, Asunción Peyra, made changes to her vineyards such as ordering the terracing of sloped plots to increase production which apparently caused a mild scandal among growers. Finally, in 1973 the current company Cellers de Scala Dei was established by the García-Faria family (who owned the building), their notary Gassiot and enolog Jaume Mussons.

In 1974 they produced the first vintage of Cartoixa--a wine that was to become iconic and paved the way for the renaissance of Priorat some 15 years later. It was a blend of the best old-vine Grenache from all of Priorat, but it's unclear if it was made entirely at the winery or just blended there. In any case, they purchased their first stainless-steel tank in 1976 (the first one in Priorat), so if it was made there it was in large oak tanks. It appears the wine was made in the traditional style of fermentation with stems, seeds, and skins. Interestingly, after the boom of the "Clos" wines that happened in the 1990s, several wineries are now trying to reconnect with this traditional Priorat and make wines in the style of the original Cartoixa.

St. Antoni de Montalt vineyards

These days, 25% of the shares of Scala Dei are owned by the Penedès giant Codorniu. They currently produce their wines from 80 hectares of vineyards spread over 56 different properties, on all the main Priorat soil types. Each vineyard has a unique character and size ranging from the largest at 5ha to the smallest at 0.2 and are all fermented separately. The majority of what they produce is the Priorat stalwart, Grenache which makes up 60-70% of their vineyards. Since the arrival of enolog Ricard Rofes they have recently started producing single-vineyard high-altitude Grenache wines to be released in 2013.

Les Tres Creus 2009 is fresh in the nose with hints of sage and other herbs. Body is a nice balance of flavors focused on being a touch round across the palate with a good backbone of acidity and a touch of chocolate that picks up in the finish as it breathes.
50% Grenache, 25% Carignan, 25% Syrah
● | 14% | 11€

La Creu Negra 2008 has a similar nose to Les Tres Creus, but without the brightness and more of a deeper, sultry quality. Body matches up to this with a rich, fruity aspect that gives off coffee flavors in addition to being braced on a nice bed of tannins.
55% Grenache, 30% Carignan, 15% Syrah
● | 14,5% | 20€

Negre 2011 has a surprisingly fresh nose with crispness and red fruits that come up in the aromas. The acidity in the body is overall rather strong and gives it a large kick that makes it a wine for meal pairing more than enjoying singularly. While the finish sticks a bit, it's an overall well constructed wine.
85% Grenache, 15% Cab Sauvignon/Syrah/Moscatell
● | 14,5% | 9-11€ | ⚖

Tasting area

Prior 2009 has a deeper nose that brings up toasted aspects. The blend spends 12-14 months in the barrel. The body is large and needs time to decant. There is a slight plush quality across the palate while still remaining quite large. The tannins pick up towards the finish and stick around for a bit.

50% Grenache, 30% Cab Sauvignon, 20% Carignan

 | 15% | 16-18€

Cartoixa 2007 is a blend of the best grapes from all their properties. It has dark berry aromas in the nose as well as a hint of vanilla. It's soft on the palate and well integrated but still pushes forward with a hearty body. It shows off a bit of minerality as well as pleasing acidity and tannins that are kept at bay.

60% Grenache, 30% Carignan, 10% Cab Sauv/Syrah

 | 15,5% | 32-40€

Cartoixa 1974 is officially 100% Grenache, but probably has a small amount of Carignan. It has a slight, light nose with subtle touches of leather. Hints of minerality and ripe berries are present in the body, but the strength of has dropped off considerably over the years to be silky, smooth, and buttery.

Grenache, Carignan

 | 13,5% | 230€

Josep Ramon Sedó
owner

GPS
41.163418
0.766234

Sedó Barceló
Bellmunt del Priorat, *Passeig de les Flors, 19*

Visits: They have a small shop (El Cistell del Pagès) in the center of Bellmunt that is open on weekends for tastings and visits to the cellar in the basement, which are free and have a maximum of 8-10 people. Other days are available by appointment only.
Contact: 650930915, 977831217 | sedobarcelopriorat@gmail.com
Languages: English

Located on the main road from Falset, Sedó Barceló is a small cellar in the basement of an "agrobotiga" that's open on weekends primarily for visitors to the museum at the famous old mines in town. Josep Ramon Sedó has been working the family vineyards all his life but in 2008 he decided to start making some wine, too, to sell locally in Bellmunt. That year they released their first vintage and, with the advice of enolog Santi Torrella, they now make about 10,000 bottles a year from their 17 hectares of vineyards. They still sell off some of the grapes to other wineries in the area such as Costers del Priorat.

The cellar is quite compact and when you enter the store, you don't even realize that you're standing on top of it until they open up a door in the floor and you walk down. There is however truth in the old saying that big things come in small packages as the wines that they produce are hands down one of the best quality to price ratios in the region. They also have a nice spot at the back of the shop with a view out over the rolling hills of Bellmunt for people to taste the wines.

Almonds for sale in their shop

Jove Rosat 2011 presents white fruits and a slight dusting of strawberry on the nose. These elements carry in to the body making for a wine that's fresh and crisp on the palate overall. As it breathes, it gets slightly spicy and is overall a quite surprising Rosé.
100% Grenache

🔴 | 15% | 3€ | ⚖️

Jove Blanc 2011 shows a nose bathed in petrol aspects. The body is warm and acidic with a quick finish that's slightly tart. A hit of minerality comes up at the end and with air it becomes more mineral and stony.
50% White Grenache, 50% Xarel·lo/Trobat

🟡 | 14.5% | 4.50€ | ⚖️

Jove Negre 2011 has a nose that's slightly mineral and acidic initially with hints of strawberry as well as minor spice and herbal notes. The body is full of large tannins, but could still be paired with many meals. It needs a good deal of air for the character to come up.
70% Grenache, 20% Cab Sauvignon, 10% Merlot

🔴 | 15% | 3.80€ | ⚖️

Criança 2009 has a touch of minerality in the nose. The body is well balanced with a bit of leather and spice at the bottom. It's initially tight upon opening, but it expands quickly to show off lingering tannins in the finish that make for a solid bottle overall.
70% Grenache, 20% Merlot, 10% Cab Sauvignon

🔴 | 15.5% | 7€ | ⚖️

Toni Romero
owner

GPS
41.163796
0.766111

Solà Classic
Bellmunt del Priorat, *Carrer Nou, 15*

Visits: They offer a taste and visit to the vineyards for 8€ per person as well as the option to have breakfast in the vineyards for 20€ per person with a minimum of two people. They also have a rural house for rent in Bellmunt (www.riumontsant.com). Call for details and reservations.
Contact: 977831134,686115104 | info@solaclassic.com
Website: www.solaclassic.com

Toni Romero's father-in-law Josep Barceló has been working his family vineyards in Bellmunt del Priorat all his life, even during the successive waves of people left the hardships of Priorat to find an easier life elsewhere. He was selling all his grapes to the local collective winery but in 2004 the family decided to start making their own wines, with Josep continuing in charge of the viticulture and Toni managing the cellar. They made their first few vintages in cellar space they rented at another winery in town and then in 2011 they built their own cellar in the basement of the family house. From these facilities they've been producing about 25,000 bottles a year, with the help of enolog Mar Sentís.

Their wines are made from certified organic grapes that come from about 9 hectares of vineyards, most of which are native varietals Carignan and Hairy Grenache that used to be planted together in the same plots. The large property from which they harvest is a historical estate of 30ha and they pay tribute to it on their bottles with the "1777" printed on them. While the old masia, Mas Hereu has its foundations on Roman ruins, there are written records of a large expansion of the farmhouse happening that year.

The wines they produce from this historic land are quite fresh overall, going back to the roots of the wine tradition in the region. The "Classic" in the name of their winery refers to that style of winemaking in Priorat and Solà refer to the sun-facing position of their vineyards that gives them their unique character.

Solà 2 Classic Blanc 2011 has a light nose with a touch of lemon peel, and bright, citric aromas. It's quite mellow and balanced in the mouth with an acidity that slowly emerges. It stays relatively crisp with a soft, muted texture that is refreshing in to the finish. With time, it gets more robust in flavors but stays true to its core freshness. It's easily one of the most easy to drink whites from Priorat.
90% Macabeu, 10% White Grenache/Muscat

 | 14% | 7-9€

Solà 2 Classic Negre 2010 has a nose with slight minerality to it. The body is sweeter than others in the area with an underlying acidity that's braced by a cola aspect. It's friendly, approachable and a great choice for meal pairings.
55% Carignan, 45% Grenache

 | 14% | 7-9€ |

Solà Classic 2010 is made with grapes from 50-70 year old vineyards. It has a bright, fresh nose that translates directly in to the bottle with a healthy addition of minerality. It pulls out in to a similarly fresh finish with a touch of lingering acidity that leaves the mouth clean and open, feeling healthy and awake.
57% Genache, 43% Carignan

 | 14% | 12-15€ |

Vinyes Josep 2007 opens with a nose that's fresh and stony but also a bit moody with a mix of small tobacco aromas and chocolate, in what's best described as fresh rain on the earth. The body shows more acidity than others due to the 12 months in the barrel. It has earthy and vanilla elements that appear as well as the fresh rain elements from the nose. Again, like their flagship line, it leaves the palate refreshed, happy, and ready for more. Despite the general largeness it would still be well suited for meals.
60% Carignan, 40% Grenache

 | 14% | 18-25€

T41 is a project started in 2007 by Albert Costa, the young enolog at Vall Llach in Porrera who also worked a few harvests in California and Australia. He says that in Priorat the real enolog is the llicorella stone, so all he has to do is put together grapes he purchases from local Porrera growers in the "Tank 41" at the winery, thus the name. The grapes come from growers typically selling to Vall Llach but that the winery ends up not using in their blends, so Albert thought he had to do something with them.

It's a wine that he's designed to be very approachable and easy to drink for just about anyone, while being true to the Priorat terroir, combining both tradition and modernity. Despite it being something he does on the side, he's able to produce over 15,000 bottles a year that he sells not only in Spain but also Japan, Germany, and others.

In addition to his T41 wine, Albert has also recently started a new venture with his twin brother Ernest, who is a pharmacist. It's a line of natural cosmetic products named Clos d'Alè and made with oils extracted from grape skins and stems from Vall Llach.

Albert Costa
owner & enolog

T41

Porrera, *Clos L'Asentiu, Carrer del Pont, 9*

Visits: Not currently open for public visits
Contact: 977828244 | albert@vallllach.com
Website: www.tina41.com

T41 2009 has a dark, dusty nose with a touch of minerality and ripe figs. The body holds minerality and darker fruits that, along with the tannins, smooth out and get quite plush as it gets a bit of air. Immediately approachable out of the bottle, it breathes quite well and will happily pair with meals or be had on its own.

20% Grenache, 35% Carignan, 15% Cab Sauvignon, 20% Syrah, 10% Merlot

● | 14,5% | 12€ | ⚖ | ★

Salvador Borràs
owner

GPS
41.249237
0.8739

Tane
Poboleda, *Mas Borràs*

Visits: There is no cost for a visit, but they need to be contacted before to make a reservation.
Contact: 607338811, 627568009 | info@tanevins.com
Website: www.tanevins.com

One of the three wineries located in the Barranc de la Bruixa area or, "Witch's Gorge" off the road to Cornudella from the south, Tane is a new project by the Borràs family of Poboleda. They named it after a Tahitian god who created precious black pearls, which reminded them of the grapes of Priorat. After four generations growing grapes, which they sold to other wineries in Priorat, in 2009 they decided to build a modern cellar on the property to start making their own wines.

With a mix of their young and old vines they currently make three wines from 22 hectarees of vineyards where they have Carignan, Grenache, Cabernet Sauvignon, Petit Verdot, and Syrah. One of these is a beautiful 70 year-old Carignan vineyard planted by one of their ancestors on the slope of a mountain near the Mas Borràs home.

They also have two Cavas which are produced in collaboration with the Castelo de Pedregosa winery in Sant Sadurní d'Anoia over in Penedès. Elisabet Borràs, the youngest generation of the Borràs family, is their enolog alongside Rubén Pedregosa.

Old, sloped vineyards

Jove Coster 2009 has a nose that comes up rather deep and complex, but them leads in to a much lighter bodied wine with a defined acidity to it that carries in to the finish. Good for meals and general easy drinking with a very agreeable character overall.
100% Carignan

● | 13,5% | 8€

Heretat de la Finca 2009 gives off a deeper nose that shows the aging. The body is again light, but with a soft, acidic backbone to it. Delicate in the body, it needs a touch of time to open up and let all the aspects of the wine be exposed, but would pair well with many dishes and provide for a bottle with depth for the meal.
100% Carignan

● | 13,5% | 11€

Coster de l'Avi 2005 opens with a well defined nose with hints of cedar and more developed minerality. Despite the aging and the general angle of the wine to be a reserve bottle, it still carries a pronounced acidity that plays very well with the overall character of the wine to make it food friendly. The finish lingers slightly, but only picking up the best elements of the body.
40% Grenache, 25% Carignan, 20% Cab Sauvignon, 15% Syrah

● | 14% | 15€

Ramon Farré
manager & enolog

GPS
41.224436
0.779127

Terra de Verema
La Vilella Alta, *Carrer les Eres*

Visits: Not currently open for public visits
Contact: 607421310 | info@terradeverema.com
Website: www.terradeverema.com

In La Vilella Alta, Terra de Verema has made their home since 2007. They currently harvest from about 10 hectares mainly in the La Vilella Alta and La Vilella Baixa areas. With these they produce approximately 25,000 bottles a year total, including the two new wines just released this year.

While the winery focuses more on function over form, they've done a great deal to make it home and get it in to line with owner, Francesc Nicolàs and enolog Ramon Farré's desired direction for the wines. As such, Ramon discovered that a "ley line" passes through the cellar and he placed two crystals to focus the potential energy of this. Ramon is quite aware that many people may scoff at the idea and think that it's hippie nonsense. But, whether it's his ability as an enolog or is indeed these "mystical" forces and their biodynamic methods, they are crafting some extremely elegant and nuanced wines that are true to the terroir. Ramon is a big believer in non-interference winemaking and is constantly trying different aging materials to let the grapes speak for themselves.

Also worth noting with Terra de Verema are the small amounts of Vi Ranci, Aiguardent, and dessert wine that they're producing as side projects. While not commercialized at the moment, they are all excellent.

One of the crystals

Triumvirat 2009 has good minerality with dark fruits and a dusting of figs to the nose. This expands a great deal more in the body to form a larger and quite balanced wine. It fills out the palate and brings up licorice and subtle wild flower flavors as it breathes.
90% Carignan, 5% Grenache, 5% Syrah

 | 15% | 18€

Corelium 2007 is very ripe and full of dark fruit in the nose, filling out the nose but still with a wealth of mineral definition at its core. The body is full and forceful with a well-defined character. It brings up the fruits powerfully, making it very enjoyable to sip. In the finish it lingers a good deal and would be best enjoyed alone, perhaps with a high-end cigar. It smoothes wonderfully as it breathes.
90% Carignan, 10% Grenache

● | 15% | 35€

Corum is an unfiltered Vi Ranci with a lovely, complex nose showing slight floral aspects as well as bitter citrus and the usual roundness that you find in this style of wine. It wonderfully articulates the large shift from the aromas of the nose in to the body with its bitter orange peel, dry apples, and a succulence that wets the mouth in to the finish. A very balanced and well integrated take on the Vi Ranci with just 400 bottles produced a year.

● | 17% | 60€ | ✶

Licorelium is an "aiguardent de brisa" made from the leavings of the wine pressing to form a powerful alcohol. The nose is naturally potent but full of mineral aromas that feel like they went through boot camp. While strong in alcohol, it's quite smooth overall, carrying the minerality and floral elements far, far in to the finish. Only 600 bottles made.
40% | 60€

TERRA DE VEREMA

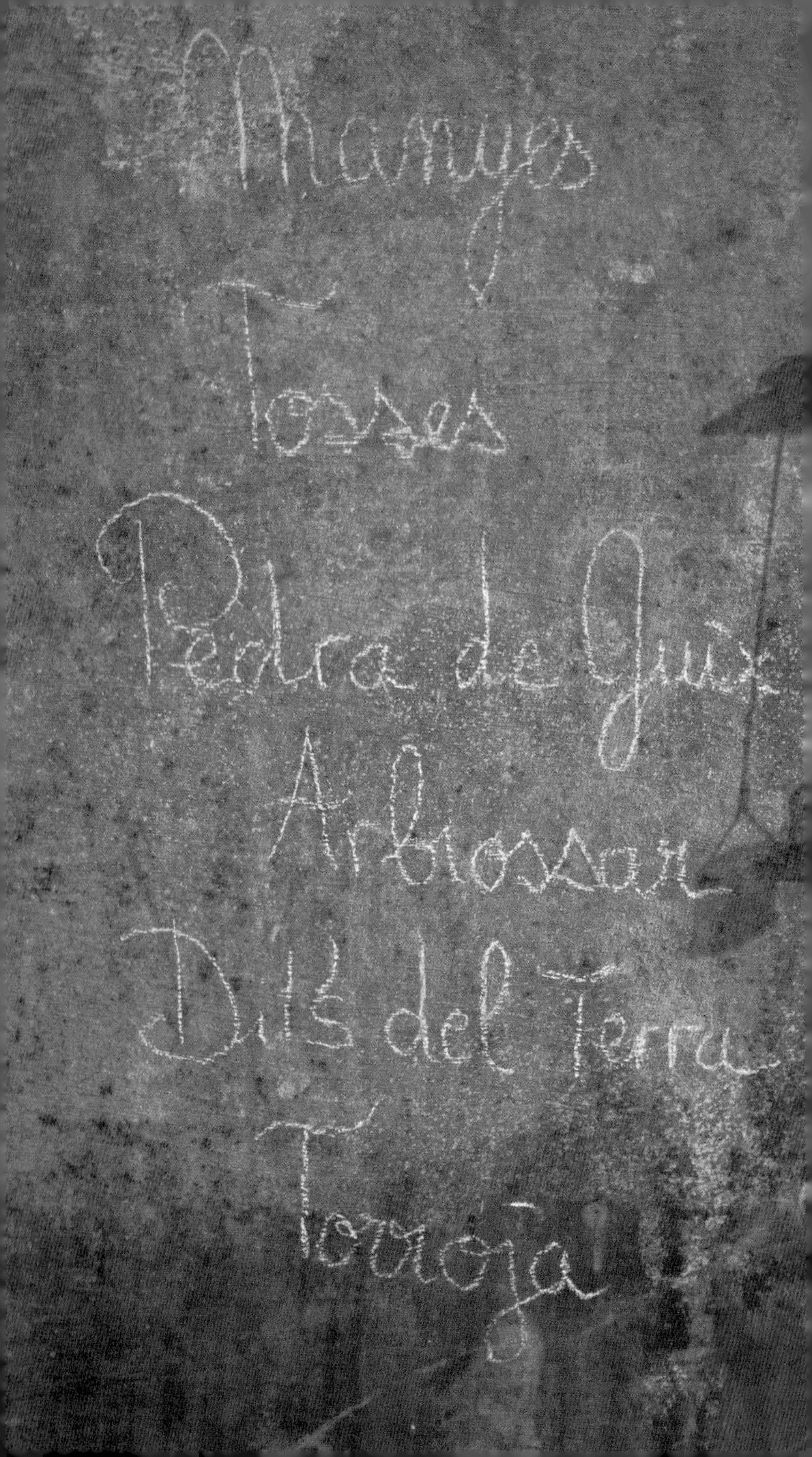

Manyes

Tosses

Pedra de Guix

Arbiossar

Dits del Terra

Torroja

Dominik Huber
owner & enolog

GPS
41.212293
0.811824

Terroir al Límit
Torroja del Priorat, *Carrer de Baixa Font, 12*

Visits: On a limited basis, they have visits of the cellar and tastings of the wines. Visits are free with wine purchase, but call for detailed pricing and availability. Call for full details and to reserve a time.
Contact: 699732707 | dominik@terroir-al-limit.com
Website: www.terroir-al-limit.com
Languages: English, French, German, Italian

Hidden behind old, leafy trees that rustle with the slightest breeze, Terroir al Límit is an unsuspecting concrete structure that's tucked in to the side of the hill upon which the village is perched above.

Their first vintage was in 2001 with only 7,000 bottles, but it was five years prior to this that Dominik Huber arrived in Priorat and fell in love with the region. He learned the craft of winemaking by working at Cims de Porrera and Mas Martinet, and met highly regarded South African winemaker, Eben Sadie. They ultimately became partners, alongside local grower Jaume Sabaté, to start the winery.

These days, they're producing 25,000 bottles a year from 15 hectares of land spread across six properties. Dominik has worked hard to not make highly concentrated, "old" Priorat wines and he strives to reach the bar set by the very name of the winery.

Barrels in the cellar

They work all their vineyards organically and biodynamically, using mules to plow the oldest plots. Dominik says they want to make wines that are very free in the tanks, with little interference. They're focusing on making honest, direct wines that show the locale and when drank, they give energy to you and don't take it away.

This is all part of a newer approach to the Priorat wines that is seen in only a handful of wineries. It can be a large departure for those used to the older style of big, bold wines, but producers like Terroir al Límit and the others show that it is not only possible, but also fits the locale quite well.

A wine's happy home

Terra de Cuques 2011 starts with a mix up of minerality and green apple elements in the nose, the latter of which initially come in to the palate. It's immediately crisp and lively with acidity in the body as well. Overall, it's very clean and fresh and leaves a great finish. Very versatile and approachable overall while still being a wonderfully tasty white.

80% Pedro Ximénez, 20% Muscat

 | 13% | 29€

Pedra de Guix 2011 spends one year in the barrel. It is quite soft and buttery in the nose with a good deal of minerality. It has a bright body with a lingering acidity on the finish. As it decants, the smallest citric and herbal elements come in to play, but they stay light and downplayed overall.

30% White Grenache, 30% P. Ximénez, 30% Macabeu

 | 13,5% | 54€ | ✹

Torroja 2010 has pleasant red fruits in both the nose and the body. Touches of dried fruits pick up as it decants. Well balanced with a dry finish that picks up the bottle's finely crafted elements.

50% Grenache, 50% Carignan

 | 13,5% | 28€ |

Arbossar 2010 presents a very light nose with a less striking up front character. The body is bright, fresh, and while it could easily drift to heavy aspects given the makeup of the wine, it stays light and delicate across the palate and in to the finish.

100% Carignan

 | 14% | 54€ | ✹

Dits del Terra 2010 has nearly bottomless aromas that sit in the glass, swirling around until inhaled. It carries dark fruits up in to the nose which then drifts in to the body. Balanced across the palate, it carries a larger degree of spices than the other wines, but isn't the least bit hot or overtly peppery. It lingers wonderfully in the mouth as it carries out in to the finish.

100% Carignan

● | 14% | 54€ | ✱

Les Manyes 2010 has a nose that's wonderfully deep and profound with underlying licorice and slate elements that give a great minerality to it. The body is fantastic and complex while easily a composition that everyone would be able to immediately enjoy. While it's large bodied and can start out a little tight, it opens wonderfully, blossoming throughout drinking the wine.

100% Grenache

● | 14% | 180€

Les Tosses 2010 has the largest aromas in the nose of all the wines that gives off immediate dark spices. The body is flavorful and like a four course meal with a deepness to it that keeps giving back and feeding you as you drink it. As it opens more and gets additional time in the glass, herbaceous qualities become more present that carry in to the finish and stay on the palate.

100% Carignan

● | 14.5% | 180€

GPS
41.190281
0.745266

Torres Priorat
El Lloar, *Finca la Solteta*

Visits: They have visits, regular tastings, and vertical tastings for 1-25 people with a varying price depending on the group size. They prefer people to visit Monday to Saturday. Call or use their website for reservations and options.
Contact: 938177568,938177330,678192095 | torrespriorat@torres.es
Website: www.torres.es
Languages: English

The Torres name should be familiar to anyone interested in the wines of Catalonia and Spain. With wineries around the world and over five generations producing wine since 1870, this family has built an impressive and wide-ranging portfolio that is distributed in more than 150 countries.

In 1996, as part of their quest to establish themselves in esteemed regions around the world, they arrived in Priorat and purchased 65 hectares in Porrera and 35 in El Lloar to start planting the local varietals of Carignan and Grenache. After nine years building terrases, they finally started making wine in this winery managed by Mireia Torres Maczassek, the enolog daughter of famed Miguel A. Torres.

Despite the Porrera vineyard eventually becoming the largest in all of Priorat, they still buy additional grapes from other growers in El Lloar, Bellmunt, and Porrera--and all of them are elaborated separately according to the plot and varietal. In total, they produce about between 122 and 144,000 bottles a year between their two wines that are well regarded by critics.

They came firmly ready to invest in the region as the cellar they constructed at the vineyard in El Lloar, designed by Miquel Espinet, was conceived from the start with sustain-

Their massive barrel cellar

ability in mind. As the property has no electricity, they installed solar panels that power the winery throughout the year except during harvest where they augment them with a generator. The greater portion of the winery was built underground to mitigate the need to heat or cool it and their entire production is gravity fed to reduce the need to use pumps in addition to the belief that not pumping leaves the wine undisturbed and prevents oxidation. They also built an onsite water treatment plant to reuse water.

The winery impresses the visitor as being an angular, modern structure with all the amenities. The barrel aging cellar is striking purely on the scale of seeing 1,000 barrels lined up. But, upstairs they have a very comfortable tasting area where they welcome guests for their visits, tastings, and buying the wines.

Salmos 2010 has a nose that shows red fruits that are rather light and small hints of ginger and watercress as it breathes. The body is larger with the oak. It's spicy with a touch of plum and larger tannins that come along in to the finish. The generally mild character overall would allow for many food pairings. They find about five years to be the peak age.
50% Carignan, 30% Grenache, 20% Syrah

● | 14,5% | 19€

Perpetual 2010 blends Carignan from 80-100 year-old vines with Grenache. The nose has touches of leather and a general deepness to it with blackberry and vanilla comes up as it breathes. There are small aromas of prunes and black olives. Te body is large, but smooth and textured. Touches of tar and cedar come up, but all built around a structured elegance that carries in to the finish. The finish is the most interesting part as the sweeter elements from the body linger forever in the mouth.
90% Carignan, 10% Grenache

● | 15% | 41€

This is an interesting project by Dic Duran in partnership with his brother Eduard who owns a small vineyard in the Coma d'en Romeu area in Porrera. Dic has worked at Cims de Porrera since the early days but he wanted to create something more personal of his own. The first vintage was in 2000, of just a few hundred bottles, and these days he makes about 1,500 bottles a year. They use organic and biodynamic methods in their vineyard, which has a 60% inclination and some vines that are nearly 100 years old.

As it's a wine close to him, Dic tries different approaches to bringing out the best out of the wine. For instance, he has a large tank in his home where he has put 60 bottles from each vintage for the last three years to age them in an undisturbed environment. Apparently, when blind tasted against the non-water aged wines, they are of an even higher quality. In the future he wants to try other experiments such as chromo therapy to see how aging environments can alter the wine. Dic is one of the most experimental winemakers in the area, but it seems that whatever he tries, he consistently turns out one of the more complex and fantastic small craft wines to be found.

Dic Duran
owner & enolog

Trosset
Porrera

Visits: Not currently open for public visits
Contact: 650968910 | eduransanchez@gmail.com

Trosset 2009 has a strong, dark fruit nose that almost drifts to raisins. Overall quite mineral in character, there is a touch of violet at the bottom of it and the aromas nearly seem alive due to how complex they are. The body is buttery with the dark fruits again coming in to play along with a soft cocoa that develops. It doesn't stop with this and stony, mineral elements come in and out of it as well as a small touch of acidity comes up in the finish. The wine is vibrant, exciting, and one of the most fascinating bottles in the region that should be had solely on its own to fully appreciate it.

60% Carignan, 20% Grenache, 20% Merlot/Syrah/Cab Sauvignon

● | 14.5% | 33-35€ | 🏠 | ✤

Eva Escudé
manager & enolog

GPS
41.201349
0.780952

Trossos del Priorat
Gratallops, *Carretera Gratallops-La Vilella Baixa, km 1.1*

Visits: Tastings and a visit of the cellars are 10€ with a minimum of four people. They also do visits on weekends, but call ahead or email to check their availability and make a reservation. Also call to see if one of the six hotel rooms can be rented.
Contact: 607532752, 670590788 | info@trossosdelpriorat.com
Website: www.trossosdelpriorat.com
Languages: English, French, German

Driving out the north side of Gratallops, what immediately looms on the horizon is the "wine bunker" that's the cellar of Trossos del Priorat. While angular and heavily modern in design, it is also set back in to the hill in such a way as to be a minimalist interpretation of the Priorat slopes. Undoubtedly as their young vines around the cellar grow more and the structure ages, it will look like it was always meant to be there. Gazing out at the view across the valley from inside the cellar and small hotel rooms they've built, you can already feel this though.

Originally founded in 2004 by the Vives family in Barcelona after buying a vineyard in Gratallops from a restaurant owner in Falset, they started construction of their cellar in 2006 with their first vintage release the same year. While "trossos" means "slices" in Catalan, in Priorat it also refers to small vineyards and thus they found it to be a fitting name for their winery which produces wines from grapes grown on multiple plots in the center of Priorat.

Eva Escudé is the winery manager and enolog, although enolog Toni Coca also consults with them. She oversees their harvest from 21 hectares of vines. About seven of these hectares are old vines and the rest are quite young, especially those encircling the winery. Old or young, they have a 100% commitment to making quality wines from low-yield vines farmed organically and favor picking quite late with long macerations.

Barrel cellar

Abracadabra 2010 has a limited, 2,000 bottle a year production that sees five months in the barrel. It has a wonderfully oily minerality in the nose from the White Grenache. There are tones of grapefruit that squeak out as well as other small citrus aromas and granitic aromas. It's soft and bready in the body with round, buttery tones of cantaloupe and apricot. A perfect balance of flavors for a white with body, but is still fresh and clean in to the finish.

70% White Grenache, 30% Macabeu

 | 14,5% | 24€ | ✹

Lo Món 2009 is aged for 12 months in oak barrels. It's quite mineraly in the nose as well as spicy. The spiciness transfers in to the mouth with large tannins that stick across the palate. The time spent in the barrel comes through quite heavily and it could probably spend another year or more in the bottle to fully mellow out.

50% Grenache, 50% Carignan/Cab Sauvignon/Syrah

 | 14% | 22€ | ⚖ | ✹

PamdeNas 2009 blends grapes from their old vineyards. While an English speaker might think the label looks like you're making fun of someone, in Catalan this is a statement of surprise and awe putting one's "palm to the nose". It's also a limited production of 2,000 bottles per year. It has a large, fat boysenberry nose. The body is surprisingly much lighter, letting through mineral aspects. Herbaceous qualities come up more as it breathes and they carry in to the finish.

60% Grenache, 40% Carignan

 | 14,5% | 30€ | ✹

TROSSOS DEL PRIORAT

Salus Àlvarez
manager & enolog

GPS
41.188297
0.856735

Vall Llach
Porrera, *Carrer Pont, 9*

Visits: Up to 15 people are welcome to visit their cellars and taste their wines at a cost of 15€ per person which is waived with bottle purchases. Reserve via phone or their website.
Contact: 977828244 | celler@vallllach.com
Website: www.vallllach.com
Languages: English

Vall Llach was created by two childhood friends from Empordà, notary Enric Costa and beloved Catalan singer, Lluís Llach. Its founding in Porrera was due to Lluís' spending summers in the village as his mother was from there. Initially, they were one half of Cims de Porrera with the other half being Josep Lluís Pérez, but sold their shares in 2001. As both Lluís and Enric don't drink alcohol, the reason they started a winery was not their love of wine but to be beneficial to the village. So, they paid people fair rates for grapes to ensure they were able to survive in the rugged environment of Priorat and not abandon the vines. As Albert Costa (now the owner after the recent passing of his father, Enric) says, "without the growers there's no Priorat." All their wines have a subtle, fruity sweetness since they like to pick the grapes at the perfect moment which is when the birds are eating them, according to Lluís.

At their winery in the La Final building in Plaça Catalunya and their cellar in the old Cal Valdrich home, just in front of the old stone bridge, they produce about 120,000 bottles a year. The size of the cellar can be a bit misleading at first as they've renovated one of the larger old homes in the village and have three separate floors of barrels and tanks. Over time, they've been renovating the house to be quite gorgeous with elements that lend an intimate appeal to the cellar and make it great for visits, such as a corner devoted to beloved Catalan poet and longtime friend of the founders, Miquel Martí i Pol.

Aigua de Llum 2010 shows a nose where the minerality comes up as well as wonderful white fruit aromas and grapefruit citric aspects, but it keeps changes as it decants. The body is most interesting with an initial acidity, but it fades away with green apple brightness and a slightly bitter finish that lingers wonderfully well with small touches of beeswax.
60% Viognier, 35% White Grenache, 5% Macabeu/Escanya-Vella/Muscat

🟡 | 15,7% | 40€ | ✹

Embruix 2009 has a nose that comes up with red fruits and a pronounced minerality. The body is a bit sweeter with a younger grape quality that's fresh and bright in the glass. It's very approachable for most any drinker and is very food friendly despite the overall strength and definitive, strong regional quality to it that carries in to the finish.

30% Carignan, 30% Grenache, 17% Syrah, 13% Cab Sauvignon, 10% Merlot

● | 15,5% | 18€

Idus 2009 opens with nose that's redolent in minerality, but at the same time with a buttery bottom to it that's so typical from the excellent, old Carignan grapes. The body is large and chocked full of tannins, but with so much character and depth to it. All of this comes in to a lingering, loving finish.

100% Carignan

● | 15,5% | 33€

Porrera 2009 was first released to the market in 2013. The nose carries the minerality with dark cherry aspects at the core of it but elements of earthy root vegetables come up as it decants. The body is surprisingly light across the palate with the slight cherry flavors mixed with prune. The finish lingers on the palate perfectly.

70% Carignan, 30% Grenache

● | 15,5% | 45-50€ | 🍷 | ✸

Vall Llach 2009 is a single vineyard wine that's mostly Carignan with a little Grenache and Cabernet Sauvignon in the mix. It has a nose that is wonderfully subtle with a touch of dark fruits and the slightest hints of boysenberry. The body is wonderfully well balanced with tannins, acids, and minerality. It's definitely strong in the body, but is a potent, definitive wine of the locale that sticks around in to the finish to savor for an evening.

65% Carignan, 20% Grenache, 15% Cab Sauvignon

● | 15,5% | 60€

VALL LLACH

GPS
41.192396
0.775944

Vinícola del Priorat
Gratallops, *Carrer Piró*

Visits: They have visits on weekends that include a guided tour and a tasting of two of their wines for 5€ a person. Call for reservations and for the exact times.
Contact: 977839167 | info@vinicoladelpriorat.com
Website: www.vinicoladelpriorat.com
Languages: English

This cooperative of vine and olive growers was born in 1991 to group the smaller cooperatives of the villages of Gratallops, El Lloar, La Vilella Alta and La Vilella Baixa to share resources. The cooperative of Gratallops traces its foundation back to 1917, expanded in 1960 and currently hosts the wine production of the Vinícola while the olive oil press and facilities are hosted in La Vilella Alta.

They now have 125 vine growers as members with a total of 120 hectares of vineyards divided in 310 different plots and 320ha of olive trees. This production base allows them to make about 400,000 bottles of wine a year, making them into the largest producer of the DOQ, although they have the capacity to easily reach a total of one million liters of wine. Given the large production, they export quite heavily with more than 70% of their wine finding its way outside of Spain. They are able to maintain a price point for the wines that's quite reasonable and even if you encounter them on the West Coast of the United States, a bottle of Onix will never break your wallet.

While the winery portion of the cooperative is production-oriented, their agrobotiga shops in Gratallops and La Vilella Baixa are quite impressive. They have wines for sale from what seems to be every producer in Priorat and a number of other products from the region. Combined with their tour, large tasting room for groups and their very affordable tastings by the glass that are available every day at the counter inside or at the terrace, it makes for a pleasant stop for visitors to the region. Just keep note of the hours as while they're open every day, they do close for lunch.

It's true that wine typically gets the glory in Priorat, but the olive oil should also not be overlooked from this cooperative. They produce all of it in their facility in neighboring La Vilella Alta, including the early harvest "oli de raig" which is something like a Catalan MSG in that it heavily boosts the flavor of any dish it's added to, although it's only available for about one month early in the olive oil harvest.

Ònix Classic 2011 is a young wine with a nose of dark cherry. The body picks up on this and is rather closed overall, but could pair well with some lighter dishes. As it breathes, the fruits come up more and it lightens up.
50% Carignan, 50% Grenache

🔴 | 14,5% | 7.90€

Ònix Clos Gebrat 2009 has a nose full of cedar and larger oak aromas. Tannins and acids both come up in the body and pull out in to a dry finish. It's extremely tight right out of bottle, but opens up a good deal as it breathes and becomes much more amiable.
35% Grenache, 35% Carignan, 30% Cab Sauvignon

🔴 | 15% | 9.10€

Ònix Fusiò 2010 has a red fruit nose that's generally neutral and agreeable. The body plays out with a mild acidity that, while not largely deep would pair well with larger meals. The finish comes up fresh overall.
40% Grenache, 40% Syrah, 20% Carignan

🔴 | 15% | 11.60€

Ònix Evoluciò 2009 has a sweeter nose with more defined dark fruits to it. The body is, like the others best suited for meal pairings with acids built up and the fruit elements coming in to play. The finish is a bit stronger than their other wines with larger acids lingering through and sticking to the palate.
50% Carignan, 40% Grenache, 10% Cab Sauvignon

🔴 | 15% | 15.50€

VINÍCOLA DEL PRIORAT

During a dinner with six other friends in the winemaking circles of Priorat, Sara Pérez and René Barbier IV started having one of those "wouldn't it be great if we had our own wine" conversations. An ironic discussion given that Sara and René have taken over running their iconic family wineries and most of the other six in attendance also had their own wineries.

Still, the idea was planted in their heads and in 2001 they bought a steep, 90 year-old property in Gratallops of 3ha comprised mostly of Carignan. They had their first harvest the same year and all worked together in the vineyard with the help of a horse for plowing (in the vintages after that they used a mule). Thus "Vuit", the Catalan word for the number eight, was born. Back then most people weren't paying too much attention to Carignan, but Sara realized the potential of this grape when working at Cims de Porrera and found this vineyard to produce extraordinary grapes.

Each vintage sees a completely different label design with artwork by a different artist. At only 2,000 bottles a year, it's a small, intimate project which is what appeals to them.

Seven of "The Eight"
partners in wine

Vinya del Vuit
Gratallops

Visits: Not currently open for public visits but If you find yourself visiting Clos Mogador (or Mas Martinet if you're a wine professional), you can find bottles of different vintages of Vuit to purchase and René Barbier IV is more than happy to talk about this project with visitors.

Vuit 2008 is a different, much younger style of wine which is in contradiction to the very old vines it is from. While smoky and more fresh in the nose, the body brings up the fruits a great deal, making it quite immediately approachable and despite the large size of the fruit in it. The finish comes up quite deep. Intense overall and grows even more so as it breathes. It's a most curious wine that constantly contradicts itself in countless good ways.
100% Carignan

 | 14.5% | 70€ |